THE TRIUMPHS OF A FOOTBALL HERO

JAMES CONNER

by
Larry Schardt

Minneapolis, Minnesota

Dedication

For Mom and Dad—diehard Steelers fans who made sure my blood ran Black and Gold.

Acknowledgments

Special thanks to Gail, John, Ryan, my family, and Steelers Nation.

Edited by Ryan Jacobson
Proofread by Emily Beaumont
Cover design by Ryan Jacobson and germancreative

James Conner photograph (front cover) by Winslow Townson. Copyright 2019 The Associated Press. Football image (back cover) copyright David Lee / Shutterstock.com. For additional photography credits, see page 111.

The information presented here is accurate to the best of our knowledge. However, the information is not guaranteed. It is solely the reader's responsibility to verify the information before relying upon it.

This book is not affiliated with, authorized, endorsed, or sponsored by the National Football League, its players, or anyone involved with the league.

The use of any trademarks is for identification and reference purposes only and does not imply any association with the trademark holder.

10 9 8 7 6 5 4 3 2 1

Copyright 2019 by Larry Schardt
Published by Lake 7 Creative, LLC
Minneapolis, MN 55412
www.lake7creative.com

ISBN: 978-1-940647-37-1

TABLE OF CONTENTS

PROLOGUE

James Conner glanced at the scoreboard. The game was tied, 0–0. He knew what he had to do. He was 1 yard from the end zone, and James intended to score.

The football was snapped, and the quarterback pivoted to his left. He reached the football out, and James grabbed it. The running back saw a defender streaking toward him. James planted his left foot and barreled forward, into the middle of the line of scrimmage.

For a moment, he got stuck behind a pileup of offensive and defensive linemen, pushing each other with all of their might, trying to gain an advantage. A defender grabbed James and spun him around. James refused to give up. The powerful running back was now facing the wrong direction, but he backpedaled as hard as he could. He had made a promise, and he intended to keep it.

Inch by inch, James gained ground . . .

A whistle blew. The referee flung his arms into the air. *Touchdown!*

James gave his team a 6–0 lead. Yet, as important as the score was, James had done something even greater off the field. He had kept a promise to a friend, one of his biggest fans. James had scored the touchdown for him.

James was introduced to the 6-year-old boy before the game. He bent down so he could talk to him, face-to-face. The two had their picture taken together, and James later gave the boy a signed football. It was a powerful, unforgettable moment for a child who was recovering from his third heart surgery.

A few months later, James visited his new friend at his elementary school. When James arrived, he was greeted with a cake shaped like a football helmet. He took time for every child, to exchange stories and high fives.

Still in college, James was a phenomenal football player, but he was an even better person. He had arrived at this moment in his life thanks to the guidance and inspiration of others. James would do everything he could to inspire others in return.

1

THE YOUNGEST BROTHER

James Earl Conner was born on May 5, 1995, to parents Kelly and Glen. James was the fourth child in the family. The oldest, Glen, was born when his mom was 17 years old. Next came Richard and then Michael. By the time she was 23, Kelly desperately wanted a daughter. So when James was born—another son—she cried at first. But she quickly fell in love with her baby boy.

James grew up in the metropolitan area of Erie, Pennsylvania. Because he was the youngest, his older brothers liked to tease him, pick on him, and sometimes even bully him. They knew that he was too small to fight back, and they knew that they could get away with it—especially when Mom wasn't around.

With a large family and 4 hungry boys, a lot of food was consumed. Clothes were quickly outgrown, and bills needed to be paid. To provide for her children, Kelly worked hard. Still, money was in short supply, so James' mom only purchased food that was needed for meals. She did not often treat her children to snacks.

A key element of her parenting style was a strict routine. When it came to bedtime, she was strong-willed and refused to bend the rules. She made sure that her children ate good food and got plenty of sleep.

Things were far from perfect at home, though. When James was 4 years old, his parents got divorced. The boys stayed with their mother, but their father remained an important part of their lives.

When James was old enough to attend elementary school, he found it difficult to keep his energy in check all day. Apparently, so did his brothers. Because their mom worked long hours, the boys were often on their own after school—and things sometimes got a little crazy. The boys wrestled, played games, and ran, and ran, and ran.

When they were given a new trampoline to set up in their yard, the outer net was destroyed on the first day of play. Two weeks later, the entire trampoline caved in and fell to the ground.

EXTRA POINT

The Erie area is well known for Presque Isle State Park, a Lake Erie peninsula with beaches, picnic areas, and hiking trails.

One day, the after-school fun in the basement took a scary turn. James' brother Glen invented a launching game. He'd lie on his back on the floor and swing his legs up toward the ceiling, balancing James on the soles of his feet. Then Glen would use his legs to catapult James and send him soaring into the air.

Unfortunately, James played the launching game one time too many. He flew into the air without any problems, but he landed awkwardly on his head and hurt his neck. James began to cry, and his brothers thought he might be seriously hurt. When their mom came home a few minutes later, Glen kept James quiet to avoid getting into trouble.

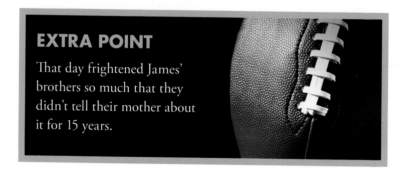

EXTRA POINT

That day frightened James' brothers so much that they didn't tell their mother about it for 15 years.

Day after day, it always seemed to be James against his older brothers. They were bigger and stronger, which often frustrated James. Yet the siblings also loved each other. James' brothers made him strong—and strong-willed. None of them knew it at the time, but that strength and perseverance would one day save James' life.

2

A LOVE OF FOOTBALL

James' family changed again when he was 8 years old. His mother remarried, and James found himself with another sibling, a stepbrother named Rico. The new family fit perfectly together, and Rico was a welcome addition to the rowdy games that the children played.

When James was 10 years old, he befriended someone else who was like a brother: Sean Gallagher. James and Sean were about the same age, and they became best friends. In fact, James' family and the entire Gallagher family became like relatives. They would often spend their days at Presque Isle State Park. They especially loved to watch the breathtaking sunsets from the beach.

James and Sean had something else in common too: football. When James was in the fifth grade, his mother decided to do something about his boundless energy. She signed him up for football. James wasn't interested in playing. But his mom made him stick with it for the entire season.

A year later, his mom signed him up again. This time around, it went much better for James. He soon developed a passion for the sport.

The North Pier Lighthouse at Presque Isle State Park

James attended Walnut Creek Middle School. He played both offense and defense for the Wildcats football team. Sean was the quarterback.

When James came home after school, his brother Michael would take him outside to play catch. He tried to make it difficult for James to catch the ball, throwing it over his head. Whenever James did catch it, he would run toward Michael as if he were on defense and had intercepted the throw. Michael would then attempt to tackle James, which normally would have been fine—except they never played on a grassy field. They played on the hard surface of a basketball court behind the house. For James, getting tackled on the asphalt often resulted in scrapes and bruises.

The danger of getting tackled on the blacktop helped James learn the best ways to dodge hits and avoid getting pushed to the ground. The rough-housing that he endured made him fearless. James knew that if he could face his brothers, he could face whatever was in front of him on a football field.

As James drew closer to high school, his relationship with his brothers evolved. He grew to learn that having older brothers meant always having camaraderie and friendship. It meant that there were people who would always be there for him. They were his role models, positive influences on his life. They encouraged excellence. From his brothers, James learned obedience, respect, humility, and the importance of setting goals.

If he wanted something, James would need to earn it. He was driven, dedicated, and determined to be the best at everything he did . . . including football.

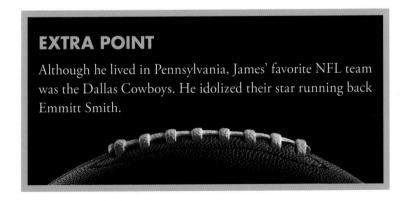

EXTRA POINT

Although he lived in Pennsylvania, James' favorite NFL team was the Dallas Cowboys. He idolized their star running back Emmitt Smith.

3

DOMINATING ON DEFENSE

In 2009, James began attending McDowell High School in Millcreek Township. He continued to play football with Sean, although not at the varsity level. Their families continued to spend time together.

On the football field, James was a solid player. On defense, he could line up almost anywhere: defensive back, linebacker, defensive end. He was strong enough to take on blockers and tackle running backs, and he was quick enough to cover receivers and rush the quarterback. On offense, he was a running back who could carry the football, and he truly excelled as a blocker. Whatever he was called upon to do, James was willing and able to do it.

He was added to the varsity roster in his sophomore year. He wore number 30 and was listed as a running back and a defensive back. He didn't see much action on the football field, but he cheered for his team as they fought their way to an impressive 7–3 record.

As a junior, James was a year older and a year better. He would no longer watch from the sidelines. James was good enough to play. He was utilized at running back— but mostly as a blocker for the team's star player, senior running back Greg Garmon.

In the first game of the season—against the rival Cathedral Prep Ramblers—James carried the ball 7 times for 49 yards. His McDowell Trojans came away with the win, 25–20. He added 17 and 38 yards in weeks 2 and 3, as the Trojans began their season with a 3–0 record.

The winning streak ended on September 23, with a 49–14 loss to North Allegheny.

James was excited about his team, but he had dreams of playing football in college—perhaps even in the National Football League (NFL). So he was worried about his role. He felt that running backs who rarely carried the ball were unlikely to get offers from college teams. Plus, he wanted to do more for the Trojans. He asked the head coach, Mark Soboleski, if he could play on defense too. Coach Soboleski agreed to put him at defensive end. James' size and speed made him perfect for the position.

The following week, McDowell defeated the Pine-Richland Rams, 28–10. James began to emerge as a defensive standout. In the game, he recorded 4 tackles and his first sack of the quarterback.

He followed that with 5 tackles and another sack against the Shaler Area Titans. But the Trojans fell, 41–28, dropping their record to 4–2.

A week later, James dominated the line of scrimmage on defense. He recorded 11 tackles, including 4 tackles for losses and 2 sacks. On offense, he added 34 yards rushing and scored his first career touchdown. The Trojans edged the North Hills Indians, 23–22, thanks to a fourth-quarter field goal.

The thrilling victory was the first of 4 straight wins for James and his team. During that stretch, James recorded 28 tackles and an amazing 10 sacks—including 4 in 1 game! On offense, he chipped in with 109 yards rushing. More impressively, he scored a touchdown in each of those games. That included a 43-yard touchdown reception in the first round of the Western Pennsylvania Interscholastic Athletic League (WPIAL) AAAA playoffs. The Trojans defeated McKeesport, 42–7.

McDowell's season ended a week later, on November 11. The Upper Saint Clair Panthers defeated the Trojans by a score of 21–14. Despite the loss, the team finished with a stellar record of 8–3.

During his junior year, James totaled 267 yards rushing, 75 yards receiving, and 4 touchdowns. He also saw action on special teams and returned a kickoff for 21 yards. On defense, James had 27 solo tackles and 46 total tackles. Despite playing just 7 games on defense, he set a school record for sacks in a single season: 12. He was named to the *Pennsylvania Football News* All-Class AAAA team as a defensive lineman.

4

COLLEGE OFFERS

James carried the sport of football in his heart, and he was constantly driven by a need to improve. He felt a burning desire to play college football after high school. If he could get noticed by college recruiters, he believed that great things would happen. The problem was that no one noticed him. So James decided to make sure it happened.

He heard about a summer football camp at the University of Pittsburgh (Pitt). At that camp, coaches, scouts, and college recruiters would evaluate the high school players in attendance. James decided that this camp was his chance to prove himself. Yet there was a problem that stood in his way: The camp cost $50 to attend. It was a lot of money, especially since his mom already stretched her paycheck to pay for bills and household necessities. Money was always tight for their family.

Still, this was important. James believed in himself, and he knew that his mom did too. They discussed the situation and made an important decision. James' mom gave her son the money he needed.

On June 6, 2012, James drove 2 hours from Erie to the university. At the camp, he and other participants performed drills that tested their strength, speed, and

football skills. Like always, he put his heart and soul into every maneuver.

His belief in himself—and his mother's faith in him— paid off. The recruiters at the camp were so impressed that both Pitt and Eastern Michigan University offered James full scholarships to play on their defenses. His dream of becoming a college football player was going to come true!

Over the following weeks, James received scholarship offers from the University of Toledo, Bowling Green State University, and Ohio University. James weighed all of his options and arrived at his decision on August 12, 2012. He committed to play football for the University of Pittsburgh. He would be a defensive end for the Panthers. But first, he had 1 more year of high school to go.

James had already established himself as a standout pass rusher. As senior, he was also the team's featured weapon on offense. He was finally McDowell's lead running back.

The Trojans dropped their first game of the season, 34–27, to the Mentor Cardinals. But James rushed for 132 yards and a touchdown on just 9 carries. He also chipped in with 25 yards on 2 punt returns.

A week later, against the General McLane Lancers, he exploded for 159 yards rushing. He scored 3 touchdowns and added a 2-point conversion. McDowell won the game by a score of 48–14.

Afterward, life took a much more serious turn. His friend Sean's sister, Meghan, grew seriously ill. She was taken to a children's hospital, where she was diagnosed with polycystic kidney disease. The painful and dangerous condition caused cysts to grow on her kidneys.

Meghan stayed in the hospital for 4 long weeks. At the end of almost every day, James visited her with the rest of her family.

During one visit, a nurse announced that they were missing a beautiful sunset. Mr. Gallagher found a room where he could get the best view. He turned to see if anyone else was coming. James was walking toward him, carrying Meghan in his arms. Sean kept pace, wheeling Meghan's IV pole, since the pole's tubes were still connected to her. James and Sean would not let Meghan miss the moment.

Just as they so often did at Presque Isle State Park, they watched the sunset together.

5

STELLAR SEASON

James did not always love going to school, but he was kind to others, and he stayed out of trouble. He disappointed his mother only once throughout high school—and it was because of football.

During a game, a defender pulled James down by his long hair. James didn't want that to happen again, so he cut his hair short. His mom adored the beautiful long hair. She wasn't happy about his haircut.

In the third game of the season, James ran wild versus Lancaster Catholic. On just 8 rushing attempts, he went off for an astounding 246 yards—a 30.8 average per attempt! He scored 3 long rushing touchdowns and added 2 sacks on defense, leading his team to a 49–20 win.

In their fourth game, the Trojans were on the other side of a lopsided score. They were ousted by the Saint Ignatius Wildcats, 34–10. James was held to 21 yards rushing, but he scored McDowell's only touchdown on a short pass reception.

The loss began a 4-game losing skid. Against the Saint Edward Eagles, James ran for 157 yards and tallied an incredible 174 yards on kickoff returns, including a 92-yard touchdown. But his team fell, 34–23.

James was held to 29 yards rushing versus Cathedral Prep, but he caught 4 passes for 68 yards and scored 2 receiving touchdowns. He also completed a pass for 29 yards in the loss, 41–27.

Against the Cardinal Mooney Cardinals, James had 16 rushing attempts for 160 yards and 2 touchdowns. But his Trojans were downed, 27–21, bringing their record to a disappointing 2–5.

McDowell's year was slipping away. They needed to do something to turn their season around. When Erie's East Warriors traveled to Gus Anderson Field, the Trojans played like a desperate team. They jumped to a 26–0 lead after the first quarter and a 54–0 lead at halftime. Given the early blowout, James didn't see much playing time. He carried the football just 4 times, yet he still managed to gain 98 yards, scored a touchdown, and even intercepted a pass on defense. His team won handily, 66–6.

James rushed for 170 yards and ran for 3 touchdowns the following week, leading his Trojans to a 45–6 win over Strong Vincent. Then, against Central Tech, he was handed the football just 5 times—and 4 of those handoffs went for touchdowns! He tallied 131 rushing yards and sparked a 49–6 rout of the Falcons.

The victory lifted McDowell's record to 5–5, and it gave them a 3-game winning streak as they headed into the playoffs. Still, the mediocre season didn't offer McDowell fans much hope for a playoff run. But Coach Soboleski believed his team was much better than their record indicated. The playoffs would provide an opportunity to prove it.

The first-round pitted McDowell against the Perry Traditional Academy Commodores. James ran for 129 yards and scored a rushing touchdown. He also caught 2 passes for 31 yards and a receiving touchdown. He added a sack on defense as part of his team's 61–14 thrashing.

McDowell had their way with the State College Little Lions in the next round. James carried the ball 20 times and erupted for 213 yards and 3 touchdowns. The Trojans dominated from beginning to end, 42–0.

In the midst of McDowell's impressive run, the coaches at the University of Pittsburgh called James. They had been following his astounding season at running back, and as luck would have it, they needed a new running back. James was planning to play defense for the Panthers, but they asked if he'd play running back instead. James agreed to do whatever was best for his future team.

With 2 playoff wins, the Trojans found themselves in the AAAA quarterfinals. They squared off against the North Allegheny Tigers. The matchup didn't favor McDowell, as the Tigers were a perfect 13–0 on the season. But the underdogs jumped to an early 6–0 lead behind a touchdown run by Khyre Drayer.

Unfortunately for the Trojans, the rest of the game belonged to North Allegheny. They scored 56 unanswered points, knocking McDowell out of the playoffs and ending

James' high school career by a score of 56–6. The Trojans finished 2012 with a record of 7–6.

In his senior season, James rushed the football 155 times for 1,680 yards—posting a remarkable 10.8 average yards per carry. He added 13 receptions for 168 yards and scored a total of 26 touchdowns (21 rushing, 4 receiving, 1 kickoff return) and 3 (2-point) conversions. He chipped in with 298 yards of kickoff returns and 72 yards on punt returns for a total of 2,218 all-purpose yards.

On defense, James finished with 19 tackles, 5 sacks, and 1 interception. He also scored 2 points on a safety.

James' 164 points set a new school record for total points in a season. His 26 touchdowns during the year tied a school record. He also set a school record for total career sacks: 17.

The Pennsylvania Sports Writers selected James as an All-State Class AAAA running back. He was also a *Pennsylvania Football News* All-Class AAAA running back. The *Erie Times-News* named him to the All-District 10 football team.

James was chosen to play in the Chesapeake Bowl, an all-star game for more than 100 football players throughout the Mid-Atlantic states. His North team featured players from Delaware, New Jersey, New York, and Pennsylvania. Their opponents, the South, included players from Maryland; Virginia; Washington, D.C.; and West Virginia.

The game was held on December 29. James carried the ball 10 times and accumulated 71 yards on the ground, including a 5-yard touchdown. He helped the North win by a margin of 38–13.

The rest of James' senior year seemed to flash by in a blur. On January 11, 2013, he made his first official visit to the University of Pittsburgh. On February 6, he signed a National Letter of Intent, a legal agreement between himself and the university. It stated that they would provide him with an athletic scholarship and that he would play for their team. James was officially a Pitt Panther.

A few months later, James graduated from McDowell High School and turned his attention to playing football for Pitt.

6

UP-AND-DOWN START

In the summer of 2013, James eagerly reported to head coach Paul Chryst to begin his college career. He had worked toward this dream since the fifth grade. At 235 pounds, James outweighed the average running back by 20 pounds. He would be a "bruiser," a player who was big, powerful, and intimidating.

His first chance to try his bruising style of play came on September 2. It was a date of football firsts for James: first college football appearance; first game at his new home stadium, Heinz Field; first college rushing attempt; and more.

The Panthers hosted the Florida State Seminoles—the 11th-ranked team in the country. James carried the ball 9 times for 34 yards. Yet even with the support of 65,500 rowdy fans, Pitt fell to Florida State, 41–13.

At home again on September 14, Pitt faced its next opponent, the New Mexico Lobos. Near the end of the first quarter, James broke loose and ran 20 yards to the Lobos' 1-yard line. On the very next play, he blasted into the end zone for his first college touchdown! He added a 38-yard touchdown in the second quarter, on his way to 119 yards rushing. Pitt defeated the Lobos, 49–27.

A week later, the Panthers traveled to Durham, North Carolina, to face the Duke Blue Devils. On their first drive, the Panthers drove all the way to Duke's 3-yard line. Pitt went for it on fourth down, handing James the ball. He burst through a hole in the line and across the goal line for the game's first touchdown.

Pitt's defense intercepted 2 early passes. Panthers quarterback Tom Savage turned one of them into a 27-yard touchdown pass to wide receiver Tyler Boyd.

The Blue Devils put their first touchdown on the board. Then Savage came right back with another touchdown strike—this time for 67 yards to Devin Street.

At the end of the first quarter, Pitt led, 20–7. They extended that lead less than a minute into the second quarter. Savage continued his hot streak, connecting with Boyd for a 69-yard score.

The Panthers added a field goal, but Duke closed the gap to 30–28 with 3 second-quarter touchdowns.

Pitt had a chance to extend their lead before halftime. With 2:58 on the clock, James started the drive with a 14-yard burst. Then Savage went to work. He completed 3 passes for 43 yards, including a 14-yard touchdown to Boyd. It was the freshman receiver's third score of the half, and it gave his team a 37–28 advantage.

Savage came out firing in the third quarter too. James' hard running kept the defense off balance, and Savage took full advantage. He hit Street for a 21-yard score and followed that with a 17-yard touchdown to Scott Orndoff. The Panthers led, 51–28, but the game was far from over.

The Blue Devils rallied with 2 quick touchdowns. Early in the fourth quarter, Duke had an opportunity to cut Pitt's lead to 3 points, but linebacker Anthony Gonzales intercepted a pass and returned it 37 yards for a Pitt touchdown.

Two Duke touchdowns in the final minutes made the score close, but the Panthers left Durham with a well-earned 58–55 victory. James finished with 26 rushes for 173 yards.

EXTRA POINT

James' day was overshadowed by Tom Savage, who threw for 424 yards and 6 touchdowns. Tyler Boyd had 8 catches for 154 yards and 3 touchdown receptions.

On September 28, the Panthers edged the Virginia Cavaliers, 14–3. It was their third straight win.

After a bye week, the Panthers challenged the 24th ranked team in the nation, the Virginia Tech Hokies. After only 2 carries for 1 yard, James left the field with a shoulder injury. The Panthers' 3-game winning streak came to a halt as the team lost, 19–9.

The injury forced James to miss Pitt's next game against the Old Dominion Monarchs. But teammate Isaac Bennett stepped up in a big way. He rushed 30 times for 240 yards and 3 touchdowns, helping the Panthers beat Old Dominion, 35–24.

James returned to action on October 26, against the Navy Midshipmen. The 2 teams fought to a 21–21 tie late in the fourth quarter. However, Pitt suffered a heartbreaking loss when a last-second field goal gave Navy the win.

Pitt also lost its next game versus Georgia Tech, dropping their record to 4–4.

7

BOWL ELIGIBLE

Pitt's matchup the following week did not look promising. The Panthers hosted the Fighting Irish of Notre Dame—the 23rd ranked team in the country.

Notre Dame jumped to a 14–7 lead at halftime, but the Panthers came back late in the third quarter. They drove to Notre Dame's 2-yard line. There, they gave the ball to James. He sped toward the line of scrimmage and was pushed to his left by a defensive lineman. For a moment, there appeared to be an opening. But a defender grabbed James and spun him around. Another player wrapped up the running back and tried to force him backwards. James maintained his balance and slid inside the tackle. He fell forward into the end zone for a touchdown.

With 9:36 to go in the fourth quarter, James again powered his way through a plugged line of scrimmage to score from the 1-yard line. The play put the Panthers ahead for good, 28–21. James carried the ball 10 times for 35 yards in the surprising victory.

On November 16, the North Carolina Tar Heels knocked off Pitt, 34–27. James ran 19 times for 102 yards and added another touchdown to his season total. The loss was especially disappointing because the Panthers needed one more win to become eligible for a post-season bowl game—a special event that teams with 6 or more wins were invited to participate in.

Pitt tried again on November 23 against Syracuse. The play of the day came from James' teammate Aaron Donald. The defensive tackle blocked an extra point after Syracuse scored a touchdown. That point proved to be the difference. The Panthers squeaked past the Orange, 17–16.

Pittsburgh dropped its final regular-season game against Miami. But the 6–6 record was good enough to garner an invitation to the Little Caesars Pizza Bowl at Ford Field in Detroit, Michigan, on December 26.

Pitt was an underdog to the Bowling Green Falcons, who achieved a 10–3 regular-season record. But the Panthers came ready to play. Trailing by 3 points in the first quarter, Pitt worked their way to the Falcons' 15-yard line. The football was snapped, and the quarterback spun to his right. He reached the ball out, and James grabbed it.

The running back barreled forward and saw an opening to his left. He planted his right foot and cut. The entire field opened in front of him, and James turned on his speed. As big as he was for a running back, he was surprisingly fast. James sprinted toward the goal line, and no one could catch him. He scored the game's first touchdown.

Midway through the second quarter, the Panthers extended their lead to 17–3. But over the next quarter and a half, the Falcons reeled off 17 straight points to give them a 20–17 edge.

Behind James' tough running, Pitt rallied to score a field goal, and then a touchdown. Bowling Green answered again in the seesaw battle. They registered the tying touchdown with less than 5 minutes to play.

The Panthers needed a score to win, and they also hoped to run down the clock. They again turned to James. In the team's last 7 plays, James carried the football 5 times. He gained 32 rushing yards on the drive. His powerful running helped to set up a 39-yard field goal, which lifted the Panthers to victory, 30–27.

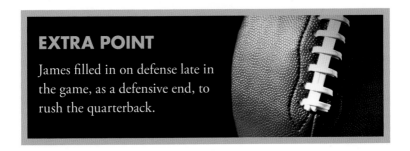

EXTRA POINT

James filled in on defense late in the game, as a defensive end, to rush the quarterback.

James' day was historic. He carried the ball 26 times for 229 rushing yards. It was enough to break Pitt's all-time bowl rushing record, set by Tony Dorsett in 1977. After the victory, James was honored with the game's "Most Valuable Player" award. He was also named to the *Sports Illustrated* All-Bowl Team.

The freshman runner made a name for himself in 2013. He finished the season as the team's leading rusher with 799 yards on 146 attempts and 8 touchdowns. Pitt fans anxiously anticipated his return for the 2014 season.

James proudly holds up his bowl-game MVP trophy.

8

LEADING RUSHER

After ending the 2013 season with a bowl victory, the Pitt Panthers were charged up and raring to go. With an off-season of hard work and preparation, James and the team anticipated even more success in 2014.

The season began on August 30, with the Delaware Blue Hens coming to Heinz Field. James picked up right where he left off in the Little Caesars Pizza Bowl. He scored 4 touchdowns and finished the game with 14 rushing attempts for 153 yards. He also caught 1 pass for 11 yards to help the Panthers trounce Delaware, 62–0 For his tremendous performance, James was named the Atlantic Coast Conference (ACC) Offensive Back of the Week.

On September 5, the Panthers faced the Boston College Eagles. James again led the way for Pitt, rushing 36 times for 214 yards and a touchdown. His performance ignited the Panthers to victory, 30–20. James was named ACC Offensive Back of the Week for the second week in a row. He was also selected as the Maxwell Award National Player of the Week.

James' incredible start to the season continued in Miami, against the Florida International University Golden Panthers. He carried the ball 31 times for 177 yards and 3 touchdowns. Pitt won, 42–25, and advanced their winning streak to 3 games.

After a hot start, the Panthers quickly cooled off. They dropped their next 3 games. Nevertheless, James continued to dominate. He rushed for 155 yards and a touchdown against the Iowa Hawkeyes.

James set a new team record. His 699 rushing yards were the most ever in the first 4 games of a season. The total was also enough to make him college football's leading rusher.

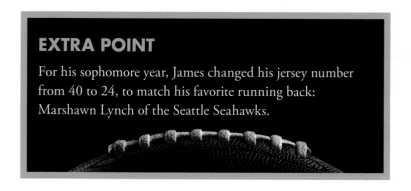

EXTRA POINT

For his sophomore year, James changed his jersey number from 40 to 24, to match his favorite running back: Marshawn Lynch of the Seattle Seahawks.

Against the Akron Zips, James ran for 92 yards but was kept out of the end zone for the first time all season. He added 83 yards rushing in a loss to the Virginia Cavaliers.

Pitt's next game was 12 days later. The Panthers finally snapped their losing streak, defeating Virginia Tech, 21–16. James finished with 85 yards rushing and 2 touchdowns.

Against the Georgia Tech Yellow Jackets on October 25, the up-and-down season continued. The Panthers fumbled the football 5 times in the first quarter, one of which came after a 74-yard run by James. The ball was stripped from behind just before he crossed the goal line. Georgia Tech took full advantage and scored 4 touchdowns in the quarter, building a 28–0 lead.

James put 2 touchdowns on the board in the second quarter. He added another in the third. But the Panthers defense had no answer for Georgia Tech. The Yellow Jackets bashed Pitt, 56–28, dropping the Panthers to 4–4. James carried the ball just 10 times but netted 120 yards.

9

CHASING TONY

On November 1, the 24th-ranked Duke Blue Devils traveled to Pittsburgh. The Panthers had a chance to win with 2 seconds left in the fourth quarter, but they missed a 26-yard field goal. With the score tied, 38–38, the game was forced into overtime.

Duke got the ball first and scored a touchdown. Pitt answered with a 14-yard touchdown run by James to keep the game tied. In the second overtime, a 43-yard field goal put the Panthers ahead. But Duke answered with a touchdown, giving them the victory in one of the most thrilling games of the season, 51–48.

James had another outstanding day, with 38 rushes for 263 yards and 3 touchdowns. For the third time, he was named the ACC Offensive Back of the Week. For the second time, he was also awarded the Maxwell National Player of the Week.

The following game, the Panthers traveled to Chapel Hill to face the North Carolina Tar Heels. James scored on a 56-yard run to start the scoring. He added another first-quarter touchdown, a 16-yard run that put Pitt up, 14–0. But North Carolina rallied in what turned out to be a back-and-forth battle. The Tar Heels scored a touchdown with just 0:50 left on the clock, which proved to be the game-winner, 40–35.

In the loss, James rushed 30 times for 220 yards. His 4 touchdowns put him just 1 short of Pitt's single-season record, held by the great Tony Dorsett.

With a record of 4–6, the Panthers were in danger of missing the postseason. They needed 2 more wins to become bowl eligible, and they only had 2 games left on the schedule. Their next opportunity came against the Syracuse University Orange.

James scored 3 touchdowns against the Duke Blue Devils.

Midway through the first quarter, the Panthers defense recovered a fumble that set up the offense in scoring position. In just 3 plays, Pitt moved the ball 27 yards to the 1-yard line. Everyone in the stadium knew who would get the football next.

When the ball was snapped, the quarterback spun and pressed it into James' stomach. The running back shuffled his feet for a moment and considered going left. A defender charged toward him. So, instead, he lowered his shoulders and charged forward. The fate of this play rested on the offensive linemen—James was trapped behind them. If they pushed the defenders back, he would score. If not, the play would fail.

A sudden burst of strength sent everyone—linemen, defenders, and James—into the end zone. There was cause for celebration. It was James' 22nd rushing touchdown, and it tied him for Pitt's single-season record!

In the second quarter, James left the game with a hip injury. But he had done enough to spark his team. The Panthers went on to conquer the Orange, 30–7. James rushed 11 times for 38 yards.

10

BLOWN LEAD

With just 1 game to go, Pitt needed a win or their season would be over. On November 29, the team traveled to face the University of Miami Hurricanes. James was back, but he still nursed a hip injury. It didn't hinder his performance.

On the fourth play of the game, quarterback Chad Voytik found James wide open coming out of the backfield. Voytik dumped the football to him near the line of scrimmage, and James took off down the right sideline. He juked around 1 defender and wasn't stopped until 40 yards later, when he was pushed out of bounds at Miami's 13-yard line.

On the very next play, James took a handoff from Voytik, cut to his left, and found an alley on the right side of his offensive line. James exploded through the hole and was never touched on his way to the end zone. It was his 23rd touchdown of the year. With that score, James broke Pitt's record for most rushing touchdowns in a season.

With Pitt ahead in the second quarter, 14–10, James ended an 11-play, 70-yard drive by jumping over a pile of players at the goal line and scoring from 2 yards out. Miami tried to close the gap, but every time they scored, the Panthers had an answer. In the second half, a 36-yard field goal brought the Hurricanes within 5 points of Pitt, 28–23. But the Panthers scored another touchdown to solidify the win, 35–23.

James finished with 16 rushing attempts for 75 yards and 1 reception for 40 yards. Pitt's final regular-season win gave them a 6–6 record, and the victory made them bowl eligible.

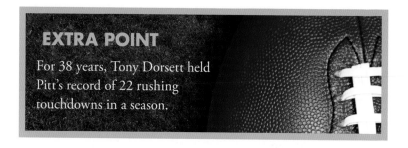

EXTRA POINT

For 38 years, Tony Dorsett held Pitt's record of 22 rushing touchdowns in a season.

The Panthers were invited to play in the Armed Forces Bowl, against the University of Houston Cougars, on January 2, 2015.

After a scoreless first quarter, the Panthers traveled 92 yards on 15 plays. James capped the drive with a 1-yard touchdown run. The Cougars followed that with a touchdown of their own. Pitt blocked the extra-point attempt to stay ahead, 7–6.

The Panthers added another touchdown and a field goal before halftime, to give them a 17–6 lead. The Panthers also scored the first points of the second half. With 5:10

left in the third quarter, a 16-yard touchdown pass gave Pitt a commanding 24–6 lead.

Early in the fourth quarter, Pitt widened their margin on James' 5-yard touchdown run. At 31–6, this bowl game was turning into a blowout. Victory was in sight, and the Pitt players relaxed—but there was still nearly 11 minutes to play.

Houston scored a touchdown, and Pitt added a field goal with 6:14 on the clock. That's when things started to get crazy.

The Cougars scored a touchdown to cut the margin to 34–20. They tried to get the ball right back by attempting a short onside kick—and it worked. Houston recovered the football at their 48-yard line.

Six plays later, the Cougars put another touchdown on the board, pulling them to within 7 points.

With just 1:58 left in the game, they had no choice but to try another onside kick. Even though the Pitt players knew it was coming, the Panthers failed to recover the ball. Houston gained possession again.

The Cougars quickly drove 57 yards and scored a touchdown on a 25-yard pass that whittled Pitt's lead to 34–33. Houston could kick an extra point and tie the game, but their offense was suddenly unstoppable. Their team made a gutsy decision: to go for a 2-point conversion to win.

Quarterback Greg Ward, Jr., completed a pass to wide receiver Deontay Greenberry, and the 2-point conversion was good. Houston won the game, 35–34, in one of the most amazing comebacks in bowl game history.

James carried the ball 21 times for 90 yards and scored 2 touchdowns.

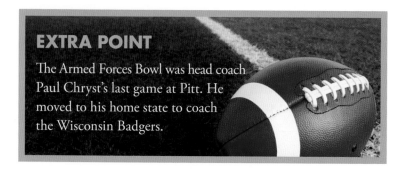

EXTRA POINT

The Armed Forces Bowl was head coach Paul Chryst's last game at Pitt. He moved to his home state to coach the Wisconsin Badgers.

Despite the heartbreaking end to the season, James had an outstanding year. He finished with 298 rushing attempts for 1,765 yards. His 26 rushing touchdowns were a Pitt single-season record and an ACC single-season record. He also set University of Pittsburgh records for total touchdowns in a season (26) and total points scored in a season (156).

He was a First-Team All-American selection by the American Football Coaches Association and a Second-Team All-American selection by the Football Writers Association of America. He was the ACC Player of the Year and the ACC Offensive Player of the Year. His hometown newspaper, the *Erie Times-News*, named James their Sportsman of the Year.

11

SHORT SEASON

James was living a busy life as an athlete and as a college student, majoring in administration of justice. Yet he always found time for his family. He was especially close with his brother Michael. Whenever James had a question or needed guidance, he turned to Michael for advice.

He made time to help with his favorite charity too: the National Kidney Foundation. In March of 2015, his volunteer efforts were rewarded. James was presented with the "Small Hands Big Heart" Award.

He was 1 of 22 college football players selected to the 2015 Allstate AFCA Good Works Team. The honor was in recognition of his positive impact on others and on the community.

On the football field, James was excited to get back to work. After the upcoming season, he would be eligible to play in the National Football League—a dream that he had been working toward for most of his life. He was among the best running backs in college, and some experts believed that he would be a top NFL prospect.

His junior season began against the Youngstown State University Penguins on September 5. It was Pat Narduzzi's debut as Pitt's new head coach. Narduzzi knew

Youngstown State well. He grew up in Youngstown, Ohio, and played football at Youngstown State for a year. His father had coached the Penguins from 1975 to 1985.

That didn't mean Narduzzi's Panthers would go easy on his old team. The Panthers got off to a solid start, behind James' power running. On Pitt's second possession, James rushed 4 times and caught 1 pass, combining for 69 total yards. He capped the series with a 13-yard touchdown run.

James ran in another touchdown in the first quarter, giving his team a 14–3 lead. Astoundingly, it was his 36th career touchdown. It tied him with LeSean McCoy and Ray Graham for most touchdowns at Pitt—and James was only a few plays into the beginning of his junior year.

Four minutes into the second quarter, James' number was called on a 2nd-and-7 play at the Penguins' 41-yard line. Pitt's leading rusher took a handoff and ran around the right side of the offensive line. He spun to avoid a tackler and then knifed forward. Nine yards later, a defender grabbed his right leg and dragged him down to the ground.

James instantly felt pain in his right knee. It didn't hurt much, so he trotted off the field. Pitt's medical team decided to play it safe. They had him sit out the rest of the game.

In just over a quarter of play, James tallied 8 carries and 1 reception for 84 all-purpose yards. Even without him, the Panthers managed to squeak out a win, 45–37.

After the game, all eyes were on Pitt's star player. Teammates, fans, and members of the media wanted to know what was wrong with James. Coach Narduzzi and James assured everyone that the injury was minor.

They were wrong. Two days later, the coach announced the crushing news: James had torn the medial collateral ligament (MCL) in his knee. The injury would require surgery, and James would be out for the rest of the season.

Almost before he could even get going, James' season evaporated. He didn't want to let his teammates and coaches down, but there was nothing else he could do. Were his NFL hopes and dreams gone, as well?

Maybe for somebody else, they would be—but not for James. After his operation, he began his road to rehabilitation. Exercise. Exercise. Exercise. He was relentless in his pursuit of healing.

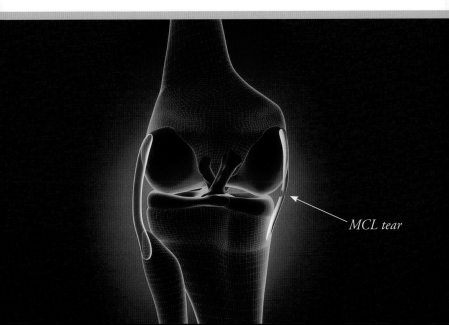

MCL tear

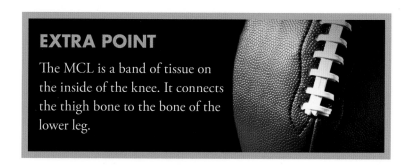

EXTRA POINT

The MCL is a band of tissue on the inside of the knee. It connects the thigh bone to the bone of the lower leg.

The following Saturday marked the first time ever that James couldn't take part in the action on the field. He had to stay at home and watch his team play against Akron on TV. It was bittersweet. It was heartbreaking not to be there, helping his team, but at least he got to see the Panthers defeat the Zips, 24–7.

Although Pitt missed James, their successful streak continued. The Panthers kept winning games, and they ended their regular season with a respectable record of 8–4. They were invited to play against Navy in the Military Bowl on December 28. The 21st-ranked Midshipmen handed the Panthers their fifth loss of the season, 44–28. But considering Pitt played most of the year without its star runner, 2015 was a success.

Amid all of those Panthers' wins, James' life took an unexpected turn. The devastating injury ruined his season, but it also may have saved his life.

12

SOMETHING'S WRONG

Even though he couldn't play, James continued to work out his knee and get stronger. He wanted to be better than ever in 2016. September and October were grueling months. He exercised. He stretched. He was determined to overcome his injury.

Despite his efforts, the 20-year-old wasn't improving as fast as he should have been. He felt exhausted, he ached, and breathing became difficult. He had trouble sleeping at night, and he sweated so much that his blankets sometimes got soaked.

If he hadn't been injured, he likely would have ignored the symptoms. He would have fought through them and continued to play—and continued to take vicious hits to his body. Yet because he was rehabilitating his knee, he decided to get checked out.

Doctors suspected that he had influenza or perhaps pneumonia, so they prescribed him some medication. It didn't help.

More medical checkups found him trying new medications. Yet, instead of getting better, new symptoms popped up. When James bent over to put on his shoes, he noticed that his face swelled and got puffy. He no longer believed that he had a sinus infection or the flu.

His doctor did an X-ray of his chest, then a positron emission tomography (PET). This scan used radioactive drugs (put into James' body) to trace and detect how well his organs were working.

The next day—Thanksgiving Day—James received a phone call from his doctor. The news was not good. In fact, it was worse than James could have imagined.

The scan revealed a tumor—cells clumped together to form a mass of tissue—which could mean cancer. An oncologist (cancer specialist) would need to do a biopsy: remove a bit of tissue and study it under a microscope to see if any cells were abnormal.

James only shared the news with his mother. She cried, yet she tried to be strong for him, supporting him and reassuring him. James decided not to tell anyone else until he knew for sure what his diagnosis was. He didn't want to ruin the Thanksgiving holiday.

Each day went by slowly. James thought about other famous athletes, like NFL star Eric Berry, who had battled cancer. He tried to find inspiration from them, but he knew that cancer was a killer. It was impossible not to worry.

On the Monday after the holiday weekend, the biopsy was completed. James, his mother, and his athletic trainer sat with the doctor to hear the results. James' fears were confirmed. He was diagnosed with Hodgkin's lymphoma—cancer of the lymph system, which was part of the immune system.

For the second time in 3 months, James' entire life changed in an instant. On September 5, he had gone from football star to injured player. His focus had been on getting his knee strong so that he could play football. But on November 30, James went from injured player to cancer patient. He was no longer fighting to get back onto the football field. He was fighting for his life.

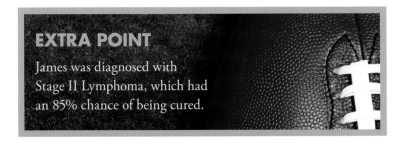

EXTRA POINT

James was diagnosed with Stage II Lymphoma, which had an 85% chance of being cured.

James knew that he would need the support of his family and friends to get through this. Plus, they deserved to know. So James set out to tell them. He started with his roommate and close friend, Rachid. Then he called all of his brothers.

He called Coach Narduzzi to arrange a meeting. Between the two of them, they came up with a plan on how to tell his teammates. Kansas City Chiefs safety Eric Berry's name came up. He had beaten cancer and had come back to be one of the top defenders in the NFL.

Berry's success story motivated James, and he became confident that he, too, could beat this. When it was time to break the news to his teammates, James showed them a video of Eric Berry. Then James stood in front of them, nervously shaking, his voice cracking with emotion. He told his teammates that he was about to battle cancer.

The news devastated his fellow players. Many tears were shed. His teammates cared so much about James. James cried, too, but he found the strength to comfort the others. He told them that he would get through this. James hid his own worry to ease theirs.

Later that day, a press conference was held. Many reporters believed that James was about to announce that he was going to the NFL. They were stunned by the true purpose of the event.

As time passed, James quickly discovered that he was not alone in his fight. Eric Berry reached out to James and arranged to speak with him on the phone. Eric offered his support and encouragement. He talked about the not-so-easy days and prepared James for what to expect during treatment—from hair loss to stomachaches and more.

Clate Schmidt, a pitcher for Clemson and another Hodgkin's survivor, offered James support via Instagram. They texted back and forth. James was eternally grateful for the show of support.

13

GETTING TREATMENT

James' cancer treatment consisted of 12 rounds of chemotherapy (chemo) over 6 months. In chemo, James was given powerful medicines to kill cancer cells and prevent them from coming back. The medicine would be delivered directly into his chest.

His first treatment came on December 8. James spent the day at the University of Pittsburgh Medical Center (UPMC) Hillman Cancer Center in Shadyside, a neighborhood in the east end of Pittsburgh. For 7 hours, he sat in a room, along with a few other patients, receiving his treatment. His mom sat with him. James cradled a football that he had been given—a gift from his Pitt teammates, signed by every one of them.

After his first treatment, James stopped at a restaurant. He didn't know that he was supposed to wait a while before eating. The food made him sick.

As expected, the treatments caused James to feel tired and weak. Yet his desire to get better—and his desire to play football—never wavered. Between each session, James pushed himself physically. He participated with his teammates in non-contact drills. This meant that he could

Pitt Panthers statue outside Heinz Field

not get bumped or tackled. His immune system was not very strong, so James had to wear a surgeon's mask over his nose and mouth during practice.

As James endured his chemo treatments, he began looking forward to seeing the other patients. He talked with them about their cancer and did his best to cheer them up. He filled the silent rooms with laughter and with comfort.

Eric Berry kept in touch with James, communicating via text messages. He warned about "the wall"—a point when James would feel hopeless and defeated, when he might want to simply give up. Berry was right. James hit his "wall" before his sixth chemo treatment. Fortunately, he had the support of friends and family and a dream of playing in the NFL to lift him past it.

After he finished his 10th treatment, James received an unexpected invitation. Celebrity actress and talk show host Ellen DeGeneres wanted James to be a guest on her television show.

He appeared *The Ellen DeGeneres Show*, on April 21— where another surprise awaited him. Ellen had secretly arranged for Eric Berry to be present. James was shocked when the NFL star strolled out from behind the stage to meet him face-to-face for the first time. The bright smiles on their faces and the hug they shared were heartwarming.

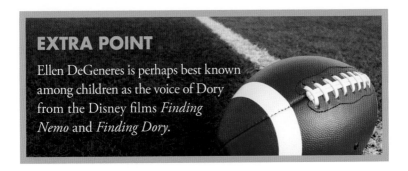

EXTRA POINT

Ellen DeGeneres is perhaps best known among children as the voice of Dory from the Disney films *Finding Nemo* and *Finding Dory*.

James endured his last treatment on May 9. After that, it would be 2 long weeks before he would find out if the chemo worked.

On May 23, he received the phone call. He was cancer-free! James made the amazing news public. He showed his gratitude by sending a tweet on Twitter that thanked God and thanked everyone who had said prayers for him.

James had a profound impact on teammates, fans, and strangers around the world. Perhaps Coach Narduzzi said it best: "For as many people as James has inspired through his play on the field, that number pales in comparison to the countless others who were touched by his courage and strength in defeating cancer."

EXTRA POINT

James' wrote about his battle
with cancer in the article
"Nothing Is Guaranteed,"
at theplayerstribune.com.

14

BACK IN ACTION

In June 2016, James was the guest of honor at a charity fundraiser. He helped to raise $400,000 in the fight against cancer. He was presented with a special award. Fittingly, the annual award was renamed from the "Courage Award" to the "James Conner Courage Award."

The long-awaited 2016 season began on September 3. The excitement in the air was electric. When James burst through the tunnel to lead the Panthers onto Heinz Field, the crowd erupted. Fans whooped, hollered, and cheered for the young man who had become their hero and a powerful provider of hope.

James' heart pumped. His legs zipped across the field with confidence. His comeback held intensity, excitement, and promise. His coaches and teammates had confidence in him. They had elected him a team captain. James was intent on proving that he deserved such an honor.

Pitt's opponent was the Villanova Wildcats. They were ranked 23rd in the nation, but on that day—with all of that emotion—the Wildcats didn't stand a chance.

On Pitt's first play, quarterback Nathan Peterman handed the ball to James. He was stuffed at the line of scrimmage and lost a yard, but the home crowd went wild! The spectators jumped to their feet and gave their hero a standing ovation. James was officially back.

With 7:08 left in the second quarter, James stiff-armed his way into the end zone for the game's first touchdown. Seven minutes later, with 0:19 left before halftime, Peterman completed a 9-yard pass to James for the first receiving touchdown of his career. James could do it all! The Panthers led, 14–0. Pitt added 2 more touchdowns in the second half.

In James' return, the Panthers dominated, 28–7. James rushed 17 times for 53 yards and also had 3 receptions for 16 yards.

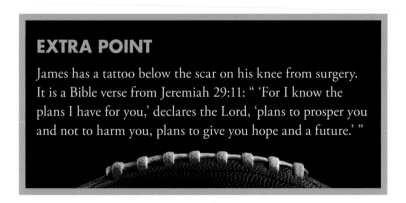

EXTRA POINT

James has a tattoo below the scar on his knee from surgery. It is a Bible verse from Jeremiah 29:11: " 'For I know the plans I have for you,' declares the Lord, 'plans to prosper you and not to harm you, plans to give you hope and a future.' "

The Penn State Nittany Lions visited the University of Pittsburgh the following week to rekindle an old rivalry. After a 16-year hiatus, the teams finally squared off again in the Keystone Classic.

It was a hard-fought, high-scoring affair. Pitt jumped to a 28–14 lead at halftime and added 2 more touchdowns in the second half. The Nittany Lions trailed the entire game, but they made it close in the end. With 1:15 to go, Pitt's Ryan Lewis intercepted a pass in the end zone, sealing the Panthers' victory, 42–39.

James carried the ball 22 times for 117 yards and caught 4 passes for 29 yards. He scored 2 touchdowns: 1 rushing and 1 receiving. In a post-game interview, he gave credit for the win to the defense and the team.

The following week, Pitt traveled to Stillwater, Oklahoma, to face the Oklahoma State Cowboys. In another back-and-forth affair, the 2 teams battled to a 38–38 tie at the end of the third quarter. But Oklahoma State scored the last touchdown of the game, giving the Panthers their first loss of the season, 45–38.

James tallied 24 rushing attempts for 111 yards and a rushing touchdown. He added 2 receptions for 60 yards.

The Panthers dropped their next game, too, in North Carolina against the Tar Heels. Pitt led in the fourth quarter, 33–23, but the Tar Heels scored 2 late touchdowns to steal the win, 37–36. James had 66 yards rushing and 64 yards receiving in the loss. After a promising start to 2016, the Panthers dropped to 2–2.

James and his team were determined to get back on the winning side when the Marshall Thundering Herd visited Heinz Field. James scored 1 of his team's 4 first-half touchdowns, helping the Panthers jump to a 27–0 lead.

Marshall rallied in the third quarter with 2 touchdowns. They began the fourth quarter with an 83-yard touchdown pass. When the Herd scored yet again with 5:02 left in the game, Pitt's comfortable lead had shrunk to 30–27.

The Panthers, however, would not be denied. Six plays later, Pitt clinched the victory, scoring a touchdown, with 1:04 on the clock. A defensive touchdown as time ran out finished the scoring and gave Pitt the win, 43–27.

James had a relatively quiet day with just 34 yards rushing, but his touchdown made it his fifth game in a row with a score.

The Panthers continued their winning streak the following game, defeating the Georgia Tech Yellow

Pitt's mascot, Roc the Panther

Jackets, 37–34. After that, Pitt traveled to Charlottesville, Virginia, to challenge the Virginia Cavaliers. In honor of Sportsmanship Week, both teams came onto the field before the game and shook hands with each other.

The offenses began the game on fire. Virginia scored 21 points in the first quarter, and Pitt kept pace with 14. At the 9:08 mark in the second quarter, James tied the game with a 1-yard touchdown plunge.

Virginia answered with a touchdown to reclaim the lead. But James scored his second 1-yard touchdown of the day to finish an impressive 9-play drive. To close out the half, Pitt scored on an interception return, giving them the edge at halftime, 35–28.

In contrast to everything that had happened so far, the third quarter was scoreless. It was as if both offenses needed to catch their breaths. The Panthers scored a touchdown and a field goal in the fourth, while the Cavaliers managed only a field goal. Pitt was again victorious, 45–31.

James rushed 20 times for 90 yards. He also had 2 receptions for 28 yards. He even came in as a defensive lineman late in the game to pressure the quarterback.

15

UPSET

On October 27, the 25th-ranked Virginia Tech Hokies visited the University of Pittsburgh for a Thursday night game. The Panthers found themselves down by 10 in the fourth quarter. They came back with a late touchdown, but time ran out on them before they had another chance to score. The Hokies won, 39–36. James carried the ball 19 times for 141 yards. He scored 3 touchdowns and a 2-point conversion.

Pitt's next game took them to Miami to play the Hurricanes. Miami's offense exploded. The Panthers kept pace in the first half. However, in the second half, they were outscored, 24–7. James ran for 40 yards and scored a touchdown, but his team was defeated, 51–28. Pitt's record dropped to 5–4.

The schedule didn't get easier for James and his teammates. They next squared off against the second-ranked team in the country: the Clemson University Tigers.

The 2 teams traded touchdowns in the first half. James' highlight came when he caught a short pass and sprinted 46 yards down the right sideline for a touchdown. At halftime, the difference in the game was a missed extra point by Pitt. The Tigers led, 28–27.

The first score of the third quarter was a Tigers touchdown. Pitt answered 11 plays later and crept back to within 1 point. Clemson ended the third quarter with their sixth touchdown of the day, putting them ahead 42–34.

In the fourth quarter, the Tigers put together a 13-play drive, all the way to Pitt's 3-yard line. But the Panthers' Saleem Brightwell intercepted Deshaun Watson's pass and ran it back 70 yards into scoring position for his team. Three plays later, James took a handoff and ran straight into a clogged line of scrimmage. He cut to his right and headed toward the sideline. A defender grabbed James, but the running back pushed him to the ground. James got to the edge of the field and found an open lane. A burst of speed propelled him 20 yards to the end zone, where he barreled over one last defender and dove in for a score. After a failed 2-point conversion, Pitt trailed 42–40.

Clemson got the ball back with 5:17 left to play. Their goals were to score again and to take as much time off the clock as possible. They were partly successful. They held the ball for 4:19, but they failed to convert on a fourth-and-one play at Pitt's 35-yard line. The Panthers took over possession with just 0:52 on the clock.

The offense moved quickly, taking just seconds to advance the ball to the Clemson 30. With the final seconds ticking off the clock, Chris Blewitt kicked a 48-yard field goal attempt. It sailed up . . . up . . . and through the uprights! The Panthers had done it. They upset the mighty Clemson Tigers, with a final score of 43–42.

Against one of the toughest defenses in the NCAA, James ran the ball 20 times for 132 yards. He also had 3 receptions for 57 yards and scored both a rushing touchdown and a receiving touchdown. The victory was Pitt's sixth win, which made them bowl eligible. But they weren't finished yet. There were still 2 games on the schedule, and the Panthers planned to win them both.

The Duke Blue Devils traveled to Pittsburgh. This was a special game because James had a very special visitor. A 5-year-old fan met James before the game. The boy was a cancer patient, diagnosed with a rare childhood form of the disease called Neuroblastoma. He was raised a Pitt

James helped Pitt defeat the 2nd-ranked team in the country.

Panthers fan and liked James as a player. The boy found inspiration from James to play sports too. His game of choice was baseball.

The two talked for a bit and shared a hug. James reached into the boy's life with compassion, gave him hope, and told him that he loved him. The game ahead would be played for the brave child.

James scored a touchdown in the first quarter on a 1-yard run. It was part of a dominating first half that saw the Panthers jump to a 28–14 lead. The second half was all Pitt. James scored on another 1-yard plunge to begin the third quarter. It was 1 of 4 second-half touchdowns that resulted in a blowout victory, 56–14.

James played his heart out for the team. He played his heart out for Pitt fans. He played his heart out for his little buddy. He carried the ball 14 times for 101 yards. His 2 touchdowns broke ACC records for career rushing touchdowns and total career touchdowns.

In an interview after the game, James was humble in his typical style. He expressed gratitude to others at the University of Pittsburgh.

16

SETTING RECORDS

On November 26, the Syracuse University Orange came to Pittsburgh for the Panthers' final regular-season game of the year. It was a memorable affair, to say the least. In fact, it was one for the record books.

The first quarter ended in a 14–14 tie, but both offenses were just getting started. Syracuse added another touchdown in the second quarter, but Pitt scored 3, including a 9-yarder by James.

The shootout continued in the third quarter. Syracuse scored 2 touchdowns to Pitt's 3. With a full quarter to go, the score already stood at 56–34. Neither team slowed down in the fourth. The Panthers scored 3 more touchdowns, including a 1-yard run by James—Pitt's 11th touchdown of the game. Syracuse added 4 touchdowns, bringing their total to 9. The Panthers were victorious, by an eye-popping score of 76–61.

On that day, James had 19 rushing attempts for 115 yards. He added 2 receptions for 45 yards. He rushed for 2 touchdowns and caught a receiving touchdown.

Pitt scored 5 touchdowns of more than 35 yards, and the 2 teams combined for the highest total points in a game in NCAA Division I Football Bowl Subdivision

(FBS) history. They totaled a whopping 137 points, with 20 touchdowns scored.

The Panthers ended their regular season with an impressive record of 8–4, earning them a ranking as the 22nd best college football team. They were invited to play in the New Era Pinstripe Bowl against the Northwestern University Wildcats on December 28.

After the regular season, James was given the ACC's 2016 Brian Piccolo Award as the conference's most courageous player. He also won the Disney's Wide World of Sports Spirit Award for being college football's most inspiring performer.

In the weeks leading up to the bowl game, James made an important decision. Because he had missed almost all of the 2015 season due to injury, he would be allowed to play 1 more season in college, in 2017. But James decided that the upcoming bowl game would be his last for the Panthers. On December 10, he declared that he would enter the NFL draft.

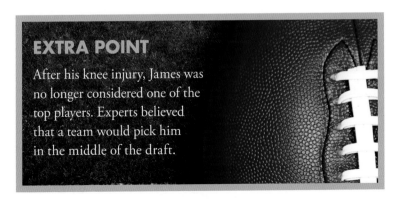

EXTRA POINT

After his knee injury, James was no longer considered one of the top players. Experts believed that a team would pick him in the middle of the draft.

The date of the New Era Pinstripe Bowl arrived, and the Panthers traveled to New York's Yankee Stadium for James' last college game. The Panthers started the scoring with a field goal. The Wildcats followed with 2 unanswered touchdowns, putting them up, 14–3. Pitt's quarterback Nathan Peterman completed a 69-yard touchdown pass to Jester Weah before the end of the half.

Unfortunately, James' day ended early. A helmet-to-helmet hit late in the second quarter led to a head injury. He was unable to return to the game, and he finished with just 8 carries for 32 yards.

To make matters worse, the Panthers lost Peterman to injury in the third quarter. Missing their 2 key offensive players, the team put up a valiant fight. They briefly led in the fourth quarter, 24–21. But Northwestern scored the game's final 10 points, giving them a 31–24 victory.

James ended the season with 216 rushing attempts for 1,092 yards and 16 rushing touchdowns. He caught 21 passes for 302 yards and 4 receiving touchdowns. After another stellar year, James was named to the All-ACC first team.

On December 30, James was honored with the 2016 Capital One Orange Bowl Football Writers Association of America Courage Award. He was also named the 2016 Pro Football Focus College Comeback Player of the Year.

EXTRA POINT

James proved to be one of the best players in Pitt—and ACC—history. His impressive career statistics included the following:

ACC Records
- First in total touchdowns: 56
- First in rushing touchdowns: 52

Pitt Records
- Second in career rushing yards: 3,733
- Second in career total touchdowns: 56
- Second in career rushing touchdowns: 52
- Third in career total points scored: 338

17

DRAFT PREPARATION

James Conner's dream was to play in the NFL. He was determined and driven to be his best. But making himself eligible for the draft and actually getting drafted were two different things. It didn't help that his final college game ended with an injury.

Each year, about 16,000 NCAA football players became eligible for the draft. Of those players, approximately 250 got selected. That left a whole lot of broken dreams and disappointed athletes.

For players like James, their fates were largely determined by NFL scouts. Every NFL team hired scouts to study college players. It was the scouts' job to determine which players were good enough for the league and which were a good fit for their team. So scouts were always checking out football prospects. They went to games, watched tapes, and used countless evaluation systems to find just the right players.

One of the most famous opportunities for scouts to study potential players was the annual NFL Scouting Combine. Every year, around 330 draft-eligible players were invited to attend the special event.

There, the athletes performed a series of tests and interviews that scouts used to assess the players' NFL value. During the evaluations, the players took problem-solving quizzes, had their bodies measured, and were evaluated for injury. They also participated in physical-ability tests.

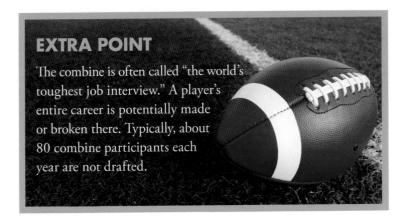

EXTRA POINT

The combine is often called "the world's toughest job interview." A player's entire career is potentially made or broken there. Typically, about 80 combine participants each year are not drafted.

James made the cut as 1 of 330 invited players. The competition would be like no other, so he put everything into his efforts. Nearly everything else in his life was put on hold as he prepared for this life-changing event.

He enrolled in a camp to strengthen himself. On January 2, 2017, he began 2 months of intense training. Rigorous daily activities consisted of workouts, weight-lifting, speed drills, studying plays, and doing whatever it took to make himself better. From early in the morning until late into the evening, the days were packed with exercise of the body and the mind.

James performed tests that measured his speed and agility.

From February 28 through March 6, the 2017 NFL Scouting Combine was held in Indianapolis, Indiana. Scouts, coaches, general managers, and other officials from every team attended.

At the combine, participants were separated into groups, based on position played. The athletes went through intense medical exams (including X-rays), psychological testing, interviews, and meetings. There was also an on-field portion of the combine. James' results fell somewhere in the middle among running backs. For the bench press, running backs' reps ranged between 5 and 30. James finished with 20. His 40-

yard dash speed was 4.65 seconds. Other running backs' times ranged from 4.37 to 4.93 seconds. James' vertical jump height was 29 inches. Other running backs ranged between 28 and 39.5 inches. His broad jump distance was 113 inches, in between the running back range of 108 to 131 inches.

The scouts, coaches, and general managers reviewed the results from the combine and took them into consideration in order to rate James.

A few days later, on March 10, James was recognized with another prestigious award. He was named the Maxwell Football Club's Brookshier Spirit Award Recipient for "courage, leadership, and outstanding effort." As stated on MaxwellFootballClub.org, "Conner has been active in the community, regularly speaking to sick children and thanking God for choosing him for this position, which has allowed him to inspire and motivate people across the country."

James had one more chance to impress NFL scouts: pro day. Each university held a pro day in which scouts were allowed to come and watch the players from that university participate in combine-like drills. These opportunities let NFL teams take a second look at players who attended the combine and a first look at players who didn't.

Pitt's pro day was held on Wednesday, March 22. Thirty teams sent representatives to see the 19 players—including James—display their talents. James had a chance to showcase his ability to catch the ball. He also participated in a variety of drills that demonstrated his balance, quickness, and flexibility.

He performed well, but no one would know how the teams felt about him until draft day. That's when he'd find out if he were a top-round pick—or if he wouldn't get drafted at all.

18

NEW TEAM

The 2017 NFL draft took place from April 27 to 29. For 7 rounds, each of the league's 32 teams had an opportunity to choose a former college player for their roster. Some teams also received bonus picks. All together, 253 players would be selected.

The first round of the draft was held on Thursday night. James gathered with friends and family at a local Buffalo Wild Wings in Erie. They watched the TV monitors all evening in anticipation of James being picked. It was unlikely to happen in the first round, but it was possible. Unfortunately, his name was not called.

On Friday evening, they gathered again at Buffalo Wild Wings, with anticipation and nervous excitement. TV screens blared from every wall. James, his friends, and his family listened as names were called for the second- and third-round picks. With each selection, hopes rose . . . and fell again. James still had no team, and the final pick of the evening—pick number 107—was inching closer.

Pick number 101 was announced on the television: Brendan Langley. James' mobile phone rang. He held it tightly to his ear. It was head coach Mike Tomlin of the Pittsburgh Steelers. He offered James a spot on the team and said that the Steelers would like to draft him. An excited James accepted. But he kept quiet and didn't let his friends know. He waited for the announcement on the TV . . . 102 . . . 103 . . . 104 . . .

Pittsburgh Steelers linebacker Arthur Moats appeared on the screen. With pride, excitement, and enthusiasm, he proudly announced his team's pick, the 105th pick in the draft: James Conner!

The Erie Buffalo Wild Wings erupted in cheers. There were hugs, high fives, and tears of joy. Proud family, friends, and fans shared this memorable moment in James' life—a memorable moment in all of their lives.

James had done it. He had pursued his dream and accomplished it. James would play in the NFL.

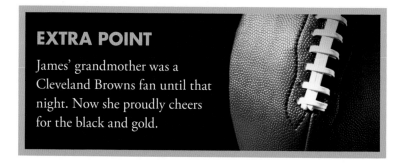

EXTRA POINT

James' grandmother was a Cleveland Browns fan until that night. Now she proudly cheers for the black and gold.

Two weeks later, on Friday, May 12, James reported to rookie minicamp with wide receiver JuJu Smith-Schuster and the team's other 6 draft picks. There were also undrafted free agents and others trying to win a position on the team, for a total of 51 invited participants.

Minicamp allowed those new to the team to become familiar with personnel and to learn the team's plays. It also gave the coaches and staff a chance to look over the new candidates and evaluate their potential.

Players watched game footage films, got familiar with the Steelers' terminology, and learned about life in the NFL. It was a perfect introduction to future practices with the entire team and an exciting time for James and his new teammates.

19

TRAINING CAMP

The Laurel Highlands of Pennsylvania came alive in late July with the burst of Steelers excitement. Training camp began on July 27 at Saint Vincent College in Latrobe. Ninety players were invited to compete for a place on the final 53-man roster. Steelers fans from across the nation arrived to show their support and cheer on their favorite team.

Le'Veon Bell was Pittsburgh's star running back, and there was no doubt that he would continue as the starting back. But his backup, DeAngelo Williams, left after the 2016 season, so his spot was open.

James would compete against some talented running backs for the position. They included veterans Fitzgerald Toussaint and Knile Davis, as well as Brandon Brown-Dukes, Terrell Watson, and Trey Williams.

Early on, James caught the attention of coaches, media, and fans. However, after only a few days, James injured his left shoulder. Doctors concluded that the injury was minor: a sprained joint. But he did miss several practices. The first depth chart—which showed where each player ranked at his position—was released on August 8. As a result of his injury, James was not listed.

To make matters worse, he wasn't able to play in the first preseason game, against the New York Giants on Friday, August 11. Running backs Davis, Toussaint, and Watson were showcased in the Steelers victory, 20–12.

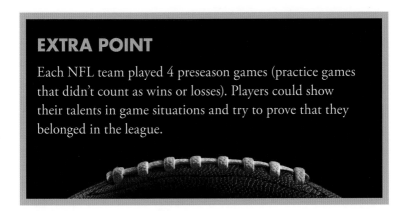

EXTRA POINT

Each NFL team played 4 preseason games (practice games that didn't count as wins or losses). Players could show their talents in game situations and try to prove that they belonged in the league.

James returned to practice on Monday, August 14. He was able to play in the Steelers' second preseason game, versus the Atlanta Falcons. James was at home again, playing in a stadium that he knew quite well. Like the Pitt Panthers, the Steelers' home games were at Heinz Field.

At the beginning of the second quarter, James carried the ball for the first time and gained 3 yards. The home crowd welcomed him with thundering cheers. From that point on, James was the featured runner. It was clear that the team wanted to take a good look at him and see what he could do.

In the fourth quarter, James helped to set up the winning touchdown with runs of 17 and 19 yards. The

Steelers defeated the Falcons, 17–13. James rushed 20 times for 98 yards, impressing teammates, fans, and—most importantly—Coach Tomlin.

On August 26, the Steelers hosted the Indianapolis Colts. James was given a much lighter workload. He carried the football just 4 times for 26 yards. The Colts defeated Pittsburgh, 19–15.

The Steelers won their final preseason game against the Carolina Panthers on August 31. Traditionally, to avoid injuries, teams didn't play their starters or key reserves in the final game. James never touched the ball, which all but assured that he would make the team.

When the Steelers released their 53-man roster, James was on the list. He was officially a Pittsburgh Steeler.

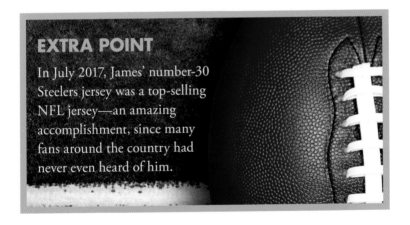

EXTRA POINT

In July 2017, James' number-30 Steelers jersey was a top-selling NFL jersey—an amazing accomplishment, since many fans around the country had never even heard of him.

20

ROOKIE SEASON

There was good news for James heading into his rookie year: Not only did he make the team, he was listed as the second running back on the depth chart. The bad news? He was behind Le'Veon Bell, arguably the best player in the league. James' opportunities would be limited.

That proved true in Pittsburgh's first game of the season, in Cleveland, Ohio, against the division-rival Browns. Rushing yards were in short supply. Bell ran for just 32 yards, and James only carried the ball 4 times for 11 yards. His first NFL carry came at the 10:34 mark in the second quarter: a 1-yard rush through the middle of the line. Yet, thanks in large part to star wide receiver Antonio Brown (and his 182 receiving yards), the Steelers garnered a hard-fought victory against Cleveland, 21–18.

A week later, on September 17, Pittsburgh hosted the Minnesota Vikings. Bell was handed the football early and often. He rushed 27 times in the game for 87 yards against a stout Vikings defense. James added 1 rushing attempt for 9 yards in a 26–9 win at Heinz Field.

The Steelers dropped 2 of their next 3 games, but then the team began an impressive 8-game winning streak. James continued to carry the ball a handful of times each game. His best performance of the season came in Week 4. On the road against the Baltimore Ravens, James rushed for 26 yards on 4 attempts.

The highlight of his day came about 11 minutes into the game. After quarterback Ben Roethlisberger was sacked for an 8-yard loss on first down, Pittsburgh called a running play in hopes of catching the defense off guard. It worked. James took the handoff and scooted through the left side of the offensive line. He wasn't touched until 23 yards later, when he was forced out of bounds at the Steelers' 40-yard line.

Pittsburgh's passionate fans cheer on the Steelers at Heinz Field.

The play gave his team a first down, and it helped to continue an impressive 16-play drive that ended with a field goal. The Steelers ultimately jumped to a 19–0 lead and won the game, 26–9.

In their 13th game, Pittsburgh played a gritty, physical contest in Cincinnati against the Bengals. The Steelers ultimately won, 23–20, but it came at a very high price. Less than 5 minutes into the game, star linebacker Ryan Shazier made what at first seemed to be a typical tackle. But it was far from it. After the play, Shazier rolled onto his back and didn't get up.

He was stabilized and taken to a hospital. It was later revealed that he had suffered a severe spinal injury. Doctors weren't sure if he would ever walk again. But Shazier proved them wrong. Over the next several weeks, he taught himself to walk and set a goal for himself to return to the NFL.

Throughout the 2017 season, James proved to be a solid, reliable backup rusher. But his year took an unexpected turn against the New England Patriots, on December 17.

James grabbed a handoff partway through the fourth quarter and battled forward for 2 yards. The play seemed rather ordinary, except James had injured his knee.

After a medical examination, doctors found that James had torn a ligament. He would require surgery on his knee. His season was over.

The Steelers went on to win the American Football Conference (AFC) North division with a 13–3 record.

They qualified for a first-round bye and then a home-field game in the second round of the playoffs. Their hopes of a championship were dashed, though, when they fell to the Jacksonville Jaguars in a thrilling offensive explosion, 45–42.

Nevertheless, it was still an exceptional season for Pittsburgh's favorite football team. In 2017, James rushed a total of 32 times for 144 yards, an average of 4.5 yards per carry. In 2018, he would be back and ready to run.

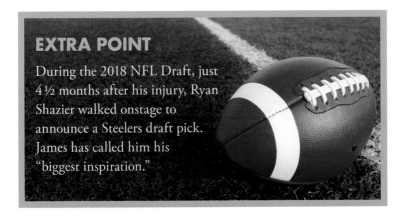

EXTRA POINT

During the 2018 NFL Draft, just 4½ months after his injury, Ryan Shazier walked onstage to announce a Steelers draft pick. James has called him his "biggest inspiration."

21

NFL STARTER

Like every football season in Pittsburgh, the Steelers began 2018 with anticipation and promise. After finishing 13–3 in 2017, many believed that the team would contend for a championship. However, one of Pittsburgh's key players, running back Le'Veon Bell, was not with the team. He and the Steelers disagreed on a contract, so Bell opted not to play.

Bell's absence bumped James into the starting lineup. His opportunity to prove his worth as a featured running back had arrived. He was already a legend at the University of Pittsburgh. Now he could begin his legacy at the professional level.

The first game of the season was in Cleveland against the Browns, who were coming off a miserable 0–16 year. On paper, it appeared to be one of the best teams squaring off against one of the worst. Steelers fans expected an easy win. It didn't turn out that way.

Early in the second quarter, James took a handoff from the Browns' 4-yard line and sliced through a wide-open hole on the right side of the offensive line. He sped, untouched, into the end zone. It was the first score of the game, the first points of the season, and James' first official touchdown in the NFL! In gratitude, James turned and hugged the offensive linemen who made the play happen. It was the only score of the half by either team.

On their first possession in the third quarter, Cleveland scored a touchdown to tie the game at 7. The Steelers answered, just 1:41 later, with a 22-yard touchdown pass. James followed that with a 22-yard rushing score, giving the Steelers a 21–7 edge.

With less than 8 minutes to go in the game, quarterback Ben Roethlisberger handed James the ball on the Steelers' 17. James lost control of the ball and fumbled. The defense recovered it and ran it down to the 1-yard line. The Browns scored on the next play.

A few minutes later, Cleveland added another touchdown, knotting up the score, 21–21. The tie forced the game into overtime. Both teams blew a chance at winning by missing field goals, and the game ended in a tie.

James carried the ball 31 times for 135 yards. He also caught 5 passes for 57 yards. For his standout performance, he was awarded the FedEx Ground Player of the Week.

In Week 2, the Kansas City Chiefs came to Pittsburgh. The Steelers focused on a passing attack to keep pace with the Chiefs' high-powered offense.

The Chiefs jumped to a 21–0 lead in the first quarter, but Pittsburgh rallied in the second. Down, 21–13, near the end of the second quarter, the Steelers scored a touchdown. Roethlisberger and James connected on a pass play for a 2-point conversion that tied the game at halftime.

James scored a 1-yard rushing touchdown in the third quarter, but it wasn't enough to win the game. Kansas City scored 3 more touchdowns in the second half to come away with a 42–37 win.

James rushed 8 times for 17 yards and had 5 receptions for 48 yards. While the result was a loss, the game helped to prove that James could be utilized as a valuable receiver.

In their third game, the Steelers finally got into the "win" column with a 30–27 victory over the Tampa Bay Buccaneers on Monday Night Football. Pittsburgh led, 30–10, at halftime and held off a late Tampa Bay rally. James had 61 yards rushing and 34 yards receiving.

Arch rivals the Baltimore Ravens came to Pittsburgh to play the following week. The Ravens jumped to a quick lead, 14–0, but the Steelers fought back with 2 field goals, a touchdown, and another 2-point conversion from Roethlisberger to James. Going into the locker room at halftime, the teams were tied at 14.

The second half belonged entirely to the Ravens. In a defensive struggle, the visiting Ravens managed 4 field goals, giving them a 26–14 victory.

James was held to 19 yards rushing and a long run of just 4 yards.

22

HOT STREAK

In Week 5, the Atlanta Falcons came to Heinz Field. The Steelers and their fans were hungry for a win, after a disappointing 1–2–1 start. The game plan from the beginning was to feed the ball to James. In the first 8 plays, James handled the ball on all of them. He helped his team get to the 1-yard line. There, he dove over a pile of players for a touchdown.

James added another touchdown in the second half, this time from 2 yards out. It was part of a day in which he rushed 21 times for 110 yards, along with 4 receptions for 75 yards. His performance helped to defeat the Falcons by a score of 41–17.

The Steelers next traveled to Cincinnati to face division foe the Bengals. James scored 2 touchdowns in the second quarter, both from the 1-yard line. But Cincinnati kept pace, tying the score before halftime, 14–14.

In the second half, Pittsburgh outpaced the home team, 2 touchdowns to 1. The Steelers secured the win, 28–21. James ran 19 times for 111 yards and caught 4 passes for 18 yards.

James' impact extended far beyond the playing field. He saw a young fan in the stands, holding up a sign that read, "I just finished cancer." James went over and offered him some words of encouragement.

Following a bye week, the Steelers hosted the Cleveland Browns on October 28. After the tie that started the season, the Steelers were out to prove that they were the better team. Yet it was a somber day in Pittsburgh. The city mourned a senseless act of violence that had taken place at the local Tree of Life Synagogue the previous day. Before the game, the crowd at Heinz Field joined in a moment of silence in honor of the victims.

When the game began, the Steelers did their best to offer fans a distraction from the tragedy. After falling behind, 6–0, the team scored 2 touchdowns to take a 14–6 lead at halftime.

Their domination continued in the second half. James scored on a 12-yard run and later on a 22-yard run. Pittsburgh added a safety and a field goal to finish off the Browns, 33–18. James sparked the team's third straight win with 24 rushes for 146 yards, as well as 5 catches for 66 yards.

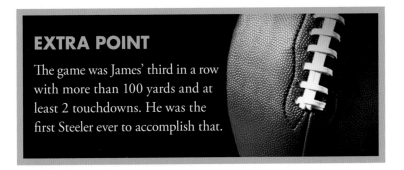

EXTRA POINT

The game was James' third in a row with more than 100 yards and at least 2 touchdowns. He was the first Steeler ever to accomplish that.

James was already proving himself to be one of the best players in the league, and the entire country was taking notice. He was awarded the AFC Offensive Player of the Week, the FedEx Ground Player of the Week, and the AFC Offensive Player of the Month.

Two days after the game, the Steelers attended a service at the Tree of Life Synagogue to show solidarity, respect, and love for the city that supported them, week after week, year after year.

With a record of 4–2–1, the team was trending in the right direction. Their next game pitted them against their third division rival in a row: the Baltimore Ravens.

Baltimore scored first with a field goal, but the Steelers answered. With the ball on the Raven's 7-yard line, Roethlisberger dropped back to pass. James slipped out of the backfield and was wide open near the right sideline. Roethlisberger zipped the football to him, James did the rest. He sprinted to the end zone and crossed the goal line just before a defender could tackle him. The touchdown was part of another spectacular game for the running back. He carried the ball 24 times for 107 yards and caught 7 passes for 56 yards. This was James' fourth game in a row with more than 100 yards rushing and at least 1 touchdown.

The Steelers stayed ahead of Baltimore for the rest of the game. Pittsburgh came away with the victory, 23–16.

James and his team continued their winning ways against the Carolina Panthers. Carolina left town with a

52–21 loss. James suffered a possible concussion early in the fourth quarter, so his game was cut short. He finished with 13 carries for 65 yards, ending his 100-yard-games streak. He lifted his touchdown streak to 5 games, and the Steelers won their fifth straight game!

James was back the following week, when his team visited the Jacksonville Jaguars on November 18. After a scoreless first quarter, the Jaguars rallied in the second quarter with 3 field goals. Late in the third quarter, Jacksonville scored a touchdown, but the Steelers answered 2 plays later, scoring on a 78-yard pass from Roethlisberger to Antonio Brown. These first points of the game for Pittsburgh came with 1:17 left in the third quarter. After a failed 2-point conversion, they trailed Jacksonville, 16–6.

In the fourth quarter, the Steelers weren't just battling the Jaguars; they were also battling the clock. Minute after minute ticked by, and Pittsburgh couldn't score. With 5 minutes left in the game, it was "now or never." The Steelers took possession of the football and strung together an 8-play, 80-yard drive that ended with an 11-yard touchdown pass.

With less than 3 minutes of game time remaining, Pittsburgh needed its defense to step up and get their offense the ball again. The defense did just that, holding the Jaguars to 6 yards on 3 plays. Jacksonville was forced to punt the football back to the Steelers.

Roethlisberger had just 1:42 to get his team into scoring position. Down 16–13, a field goal would tie the game and a touchdown would win it. The Steelers wasted no time. They drove 67 yards on 6 plays, all the way to the 1-yard line. With just 0:05 left on the clock, Roethlisberger ran the football into the end zone, lifting the Steelers to an astonishing comeback victory, 20–16.

James rushed 9 times for 25 yards and had 6 catches for 24 yards. He did not score a touchdown in the Steelers' win. But he was thrilled that his team had risen to a record of 7–2–1. They were widely considered one of the best teams in the league, and the playoffs were in sight.

23

DISAPPOINTING FINISHES

In Week 12, the Steelers traveled to Denver. Pittsburgh marched the football up and down the field on the Broncos. Yet they didn't have much to show for it. Denver's stingy defense made several big plays, including a blocked field goal and a forced fumble at the goal line. All together, Pittsburgh racked up more than 500 yards of offense— and 4 turnovers!

The Steelers' most costly mistake came on their final offensive play of the game. With just over a minute to go, the team was behind by a touchdown, 24–17. But the ball was at Denver's 2-yard line, so Pittsburgh was in prime position to tie the game and send it into overtime.

On third down, Roethlisberger caught the snap from center and faked a handoff, then he tossed the ball into the middle of the end zone. He didn't see defensive lineman Shelby Harris pretend to rush and then drop back into coverage. Roethlisberger threw an interception right to him—and Denver's victory was secured. James rushed for 53 yards and added 42 yards receiving in the game.

After the heartbreaking loss, Pittsburgh returned to Heinz Field to host the Los Angeles Chargers a week later,

James gained 60 yards versus the Chargers but left the game early.

in a nationally televised Sunday night game. James got off to a hot start, scoring 2 touchdowns in the first quarter.

The Chargers responded with a touchdown late in the first, but the second quarter was all Steelers. They added a field goal and a touchdown, giving them a 23–7 lead.

In the second half, the Chargers roared back with 3 unanswered touchdowns (and two 2-point conversions) to take the lead, 30–23. The Steelers put together a 78-yard touchdown drive that tied the game with 4:10 to go.

Los Angeles took over from there. They used up every remaining second on their way to Pittsburgh's 16-yard line. The Chargers' winning field goal attempt was blocked, and for a moment it appeared that the game had been saved. But an offsides penalty was called, giving the Chargers another try. This time, the kick went through the uprights, and the Steelers fell, 33–30.

James carried the ball 15 times for 60 yards. In the fourth quarter, he left the game with a high ankle sprain. The injury was originally thought to be minor, but it ended up being more serious than expected.

Because of his injury, James could not play in Pittsburgh's next game, in Oakland against the Raiders. His absence was noticed. Despite being favored to win, the Steelers fell to Oakland when quarterback Derek Carr threw a 6-yard touchdown pass with just 0:21 left in the game. The play handed Pittsburgh the loss, 24–21.

Suddenly, the team that seemed destined for a playoff run was in danger of missing the playoffs altogether. After 3 losses in a row, their record stood at 7–5–1.

The New England Patriots visited Pittsburgh to face the Steelers on December 16. The Steelers were in desperate need of a victory, but they were up against one of the league's top teams. To make matters worse, James was still out of commission.

Without their running back, the offense struggled to put points on the board. But Pittsburgh's defense played one of its best games of the year, holding New England—and star quarterback Tom Brady—to just 10 points. The Steelers' 17 points were enough to lift them to victory for the first time in nearly a month.

In Week 16, the Steelers played another of the NFL's best teams. This time, they traveled to New Orleans to take on the 12–2 Saints. The playoff picture in the AFC was crowded. Pittsburgh clung to their lead in the AFC North division, but Baltimore was right behind them. Three other teams were also within a game of Pittsburgh's record, so it was possible that a loss could drop the Steelers out of the playoffs entirely.

The solution was simple: Keep winning. But that would be a difficult task with James out yet again. His ankle still wasn't healed.

The Steelers played well enough to win. They led, 28–24, with under 2 minutes to go. But Saints quarterback Drew Brees threw a touchdown to give his team a 31–28 lead at the 1:28 mark.

Still, Pittsburgh had a chance. In less than a minute, the Steelers marched into New Orleans territory with momentum on their side. But a fumble on the 42-yard line gave the Saints the ball—and the victory.

The news grew even worse for Pittsburgh. The Ravens won their game, bumping the Steelers out of the top spot in the AFC North.

The Indianapolis Colts and Tennessee Titans won their games, too, leapfrogging ahead of Pittsburgh in the wildcard standings. In just 1 week, James and his team had dropped from fourth overall to eighth overall. With only 6 AFC teams getting into the playoffs, the odds were no longer in their favor.

24

LAST CHANCE

December 30 arrived, the last week of the regular season. The entire Steelers' season boiled down to this: In order to make the playoffs, Pittsburgh needed to win its game against the Cincinnati Bengals, and the Cleveland Browns had to defeat the Baltimore Ravens.

There was nothing Pittsburgh's players could do about the Browns-Ravens game. They just had to take care of business at Heinz Field. The Steelers burst onto the field in front of a crowd of 63,874 cheering fans. James was among them, back and ready to battle. Terrible Towels waved in a sea of gold.

Nerves got the better of the Steelers to begin the game. The offense started slowly. Neither team scored in the first quarter, but Cincinnati broke the tie early in the second when a defensive player intercepted a Ben Roethlisberger pass and returned it for a touchdown. Both teams added field goals, and the Bengals led at halftime, 10–3.

Late in the third quarter, Roethlisberger connected with JuJu Smith-Schuster for an 11-yard touchdown pass to tie the score. Then, with 8:35 left in the game, the Steelers kicked a 47-yard field goal that grazed the upright and squeaked through.

The Bengals answered quickly with a 32-yard field goal that tied the game again, 13–13. The Steelers responded with a clutch 12-play, 58-yard drive, sparked by a short pass to James in the middle of the field that he turned into a 20-yard gain.

With 1:56 left to play, kicker Matt McCrane trotted onto the field. McCrane, who was a replacement for the injured Chris Boswell, had been with the team for less than a week. Now, he was potentially kicking for a spot in the playoffs.

McCrane handled the pressure like a champion. He kicked a 35-yard field goal that proved to be the last score of the game. The Steelers held on to win, 16–13.

When the game ended, all eyes focused on the Browns-Ravens contest. Baltimore held a slim lead, 26–24, but the Browns got the ball on their own 26, with 1:49 to go. There was still a chance. A field goal would send Pittsburgh into the playoffs.

The Browns moved all the way to the Ravens' 39, just a few yards from field goal range. But the hopes of the entire Steeler Nation were dashed when Browns' quarterback Baker Mayfield threw an interception.

The season was over for the Pittsburgh Steelers. For the first time in 5 years, they would not be in the playoffs.

Even though the year didn't turn out the way he hoped, James proved himself as a valuable runner and a powerful offensive weapon. He was rewarded for his spectacular first season as a starter. On December 18, 2018, James was named to the 2019 Pro Bowl, an all-star game at the end of January.

The Pro Bowl showcased some of the best players in the league, elected by votes from fans, coaches, and other players. It was a tremendous honor to be picked for the Pro Bowl. James was chosen as a starter.

He was joined on the AFC squad by teammates Cameron Heyward (defensive end), Maurkice Pouncey (center), JuJu Smith-Schuster (wide receiver), Alejandro Villanueva (offensive tackle), and T. J. Watt (linebacker).

The week leading up to the Pro Bowl was packed with events to entertain fans, including flag football games, performances by high school bands, pep rallies, practices, skills contests, and more. James took the opportunity to interact with spectators and sign autographs.

One of the fun things about the all-star game was that division rivals became teammates. James found himself playing with such regular-season adversaries as Cleveland wide receiver Jarvis Landry and Baltimore safety Eric Weddle.

EXTRA POINT

James wore his familiar number 30, but his AFC jersey was red. The NFC wore blue.

James attended the 2019 Maxim Big Game Experience.

The action started at 3 p.m. on Sunday, January 27, 2019, at Camping World Stadium in Orlando, Florida. Kansas City quarterback Patrick Mahomes began the game with a pass to James that was good for 18 yards and a first down. In the same drive, James ran the ball 12 yards around the left side of the line to set up the ball on the National Football Conference (NFC) 18-yard line. Two plays later, the AFC scored the game's first touchdown.

In the second quarter, the AFC added a touchdown and a field goal, giving James' team a 17–0 lead at halftime.

The AFC's domination continued in the second half. The NFC all-stars didn't get on the board until the 9:09 mark in the fourth quarter. When the final seconds of the clock ticked away, the AFC was victorious, 26–7. In the exhibition game, James rushed 6 times for 11 yards and caught 3 passes for 34 yards.

Despite missing 3 games due to injury, James ended the season with 215 rushing attempts for 973 yards, along with 55 receptions for 497 yards. He scored 12 rushing touchdowns and 1 receiving touchdown.

He surpassed the expectations of Steelers fans—and football fans across the country. In just his second NFL season, he went from a rarely used reserve player to one of the most valuable offensive players in the league. But James wasn't finished. He believed that, in the seasons to come, he could help the Steelers get back into the playoffs and perhaps even bring home another National Football League championship.

Amazing Sports Biographies

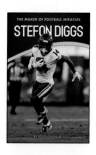

STEFON DIGGS

He overcame high school tragedy and a severe college injury and is perhaps best known for one of the greatest plays in NFL playoff history.

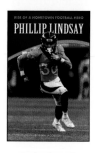

PHILLIP LINDSAY

A knee injury couldn't derail his historic college career, but when no team drafted him, few could guess that he would become one of the league's best backs.

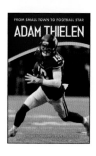

ADAM THIELEN

He couldn't find a college football team that wanted him, yet he worked his way from tryouts, to practice squad, to special teams, to all-star wide receiver.

Read all the incredible true stories of athletes who achieved their dreams through hard work, dedication, and perseverance. The Amazing Sports Biographies are available wherever books are sold.

SOURCES

247 Sports (247sports.com).
- "James Conner, McDowell." Accessed on March 11, 2019.
- "James Conner Timeline Events." Accessed on March 2, 2019.

"2018 NFL Attendance Data." Pro Football Reference (pro-football-reference.com). Accessed on May 23, 2019.

ABC News. "Steelers Linebacker Suffers Major Back Injury." YouTube (youtube.com). December 5, 2017.

"About the National Letter of Intent." National Letter of Intent (nationalletter.org). Accessed on April 6, 2019.

ACC Digital Network. YouTube (youtube.com).
- Pitt vs. Clemson. November 12, 2016.
- Pitt vs. Virginia. October 15, 2016.
- Youngstown State vs. Pitt. September 5, 2015.
- Syracuse vs. Pitt. November 22, 2014.
- Pitt vs. Bowling Green. December 26, 2013.
- "Pitt's James Conner No Longer Under the Radar." August 10, 2015.

AP. "Erie Native Conner Picked as AFC Starter for Pro Bowl." GoErie (goerie.com). December 19, 2018.

AP. "Pitt RB James Conner out for Year with Knee Injury." *USA Today* (usatoday.com). September 7, 2015.

Auerbach, Nicole. "Mapping James Conner: Pitt RB's Body Traces Path to Hell and Back. *USA Today* (usatoday.com). June 24, 2016.

Berman, Beau. "James Conner's NFL Draft Night Journey." YouTube (youtube.com). August 23, 2017.

Bouchette, Ed. *Pittsburgh Post-Gazette* (post-gazette.com).
- "James Conner's Story Gets Better, but What about His Injured Ankle?" December 19, 2018.
- " 'Our City Took a Hit': Steelers Put Aside Heartbreak, Pound Browns at Heinz Field." October 28, 2018.

Brady, James. "Pro Bowl 2019 Rosters: Who's on Each Team?" SB Nation (sbnation.com). January 27, 2019.

Brinson, Will. CBS Sports (cbssports.com).
- "NFL Playoff Picture Standings with Complete Week 15 Results: Saints Big Winners as Playoff Bracket Shakes Out." December 18, 2018.
- "2017 NFL Combine Schedule: Breakdown of Daily Player Workouts for Each Position." February 28, 2017.

Brinson, Will and R.J. White. "NFL Playoff Picture Week 16 Standings: Steelers Likely out, Seahawks Clinch Spot, Saints Earn Home-field Advantage." CBS Sports (cbssports.com). December 24, 2018.

Bryan, Dave. "Steelers Week 1 Depth Chart: Watt Listed as Starter, JuJu Top Kickoff Returner." Steelers Depot (steelersdepot.com). September 5, 2017.

CardiacHill. "James Conner Injury a Big One for Pitt." SB Nation: Cardiac Hill (cardiachill.com). October 15, 2013.

"Chesapeake Bowl." Maryland's Sports Commission (marylandsports.us). Accessed on March 2, 2019.

Chester, Simon. "Despite Growing up a Cowboys Fan, James Conner Is 'So Thankful' to Be with the Steelers." SB Nation: Behind the Steel Curtain (behindthesteelcurtain.com). October 20, 2018.

Chester, Simon A. Steelers Wire (steelerswire.com).
- "Steelers Official 53-man Roster for 2017." September 2, 2017.
- "Steelers Expecting 51 Participants for Rookie Minicamp." May 11, 2017.

Conner, James. *The Players Tribune* (theplayerstribune.com).
- "A Letter to NFL GMs." April 20, 2017.
- "Nothing Is Guaranteed." July 25, 2016.

D'Andrea, Christian. "NFL Draft 2017: Pick-by-pick Results." SB Nation (sbnation.com). April 29, 2017.

Daniels, Tim. Bleacher Report (bleacherreport.com).
- "James Conner Suffers Shoulder Injury During Steelers Training Camp." August 2, 2017.
- "NFL Combine 2017 Results." March 3, 2017.

Deardo, Bryan. "James Conner Wins FedEx Ground Player of the Week." 247 Sports (247sports.com). September 13, 2018.

Deardo, Bryan. "Steelers Sign K Matt McCrane, Place Chris Boswell on IR." 247 Sports (247sports.com). December 28, 2018.

DiPaola, Jerry. *Trib Live* (archive.triblive.com).
- "Pitt Star Running Back Conner Remains Grounded Despite Success." August 29, 2015.
- "Pitt Star Conner Befriends Ailing Erie Boy." June 17, 2015.

"Disney Spirit Award." National College Football Awards Association (ncfaa.org). Accessed on May 10, 2019.

Dudley, John. "Conner Named *Erie-Times News* Sportsman of the Year." GoErie (goerie.com). December 26, 2014.

Dulac, Gerry. *Pittsburgh Post-Gazette* (post-gazette.com).
- "James Conner to Have Knee Surgery Wednesday, Ending His Season." December 19, 2017.
- "Despite Injury, James Conner Doesn't Think He's Falling Behind in Camp." August 14, 2017.

Ellis, Zac. "James Conner, Pitt Top Bowling Green in Little Caesars Bowl." *Sports Illustrated* (si.com). December 26, 2013.

ESPN (espn.com).
- Pitt vs. Clemson. November 12, 2016.
- Pitt vs. Virginia. October 15, 2016.
- Youngstown State vs. Pitt. September 5, 2015.
- Pitt vs. Miami. November 29, 2014.
- Syracuse vs. Pitt. November 22, 2014.
- Georgia Tech vs. Pitt. October 25, 2014.
- Pitt vs. Bowling Green. December 26, 2013.
- Notre Dame vs. Pitt. November 9, 2013.

"Estimated Probability of Competing in Professional Athletics." NCAA (ncaa.org). Accessed on May 3, 2019.

Fernandes, Victor. "Conner Injured as Pitt Falls in Pinstripe Bowl." GoErie (goerie.com). December 28, 2016.

"Football Recruiting 101: Running Back." Go Big Recruiting (gobigrecruiting.com). Accessed on March 7, 2019.

Fowler, Jeremy. "James Conner Was Eager to Turn His Storyline Back to Football." ESPN (espn.com). August 21, 2017.

Hamilton, Brian. "Molded by His Family, Pitt's James Conner Rushing into Record Books." *Sports Illustrated* (si.com). September 16, 2014.

Haney, Travis. "Pitt Running Back James Conner to Appear on 'The Ellen DeGeneres Show.' " ESPN (espn.com). April 21, 2016.

Hanzus, Dan. "Rookie James Conner Has NFL's Hottest-selling Jersey." NFL (nfl.com). July 25, 2017.

Hartman, Jeff. "2019 Pro Bowl: Time, TV Schedule, Rosters and Open Thread." SB Nation: Behind the Steel Curtain (behindthesteelcurtain.com). January 27, 2019.

Howe, Connor. "2017 NFL Combine: Full List of 330 Players Invited." SB Nation (sbnation.com). February 15, 2017.

Iniguez, Alex. "Steelers Announce 2017 Training Camp Schedule." *Pittsburgh Post-Gazette* (post-gazette.com). May 31, 2017.

"James Conner Greets Young Cancer Patient Prior to Big Game vs. Bengals." KDKA-TV (pittsburgh.cbslocal.com). October 14, 2018.

Kirschman, Lauren. Penn Live (pennlive.com).
- "NFL Draft 2017: James Conner's Timeline from His Pitt Commitment to the Pittsburgh Steelers." Accessed on April 1, 2019.
- "James Conner Breaks Two ACC Records in Pitt's Win over Duke." November 19, 2016.

Klinger, Jacob. Penn Live (pennlive.com).
- "James Conner Issues Caution on Ankle Injury, Is 'Day to Day.' " December 19, 2018.
- "James Conner Wins AFC Offensive Player of the Week." October 31, 2018.

Knoblauch, Austin. NFL (nfl.com).
- "Le'Veon Bell Does Not Sign Tag, Will Miss 2018 Season." November 14, 2018.
- "James Conner Suffers Concussion During Steelers' Win." November 9, 2018.

Kramer, Adam. "How James Conner Went from Unwanted Recruit to All-American RB." Bleacher Report (bleacherreport.com). July 9, 2015.

Kuzma, Joe. "Stats That Stood out in 2016: DeAngelo Williams Edition." Steel City Underground (steelcityunderground.com). June 13, 2017

MaxPreps (maxpreps.com). Accessed on April 13, 2019.
- 2012 PIAA Football Championship
- McDowell 2012 Football Schedule
- McDowell 2011 Football Schedule
- McDowell 2010 Football Roster
- McDowell 2010 Football Schedule
- McDowell 2009 Football Schedule
- North Allegheny vs. McDowell. November 30, 2012.
- East vs. McDowell. October 19, 2012.
- McKeesport vs. McDowell. November 4, 2011.
- North Hills vs. McDowell. October 14, 2011.
- James Conner
- James Conner's Football Stats

Marczim, Matthew. "James Conner Continues Putting Himself
in Rarefied Air Le'Veon Bell Hasn't Breathed." Steelers Depot
(steelersdepot.com). October 29, 2018.

maxwellclub. "Pitt's James Conner Honored: Maxwell Football
Club Thomas Brookshier Spirit Award." Maxwell Football Club
(maxwellfootballclub.org). June 26, 2017.

Mayo Clinc (mayoclinic.org).
- "Polycystic Kidney Disease." Accessed on May 19, 2019.
- "Positron Emission Tomography Scan." Accessed on May 12, 2019.

Meredith Videos. "Pittsburgh Steelers in Attendance for Funeral
of Tree of Life Synagogue Shooting Victims." Yahoo Finance
(finance.yahoo.com). October 30, 2018.

NFL (nfl.com).
- "FedEx Air & Ground Players of the Week." Accessed on May 1, 2019.
- "James Conner." Accessed on February 27, 2019.
- "James Conner: Combine Profile." Accessed on March 2, 2019.

"NFL Game Center." NFL (nfl.com).
- "Pittsburgh Steelers 2018 Schedule."
- "Pittsburgh Steelers 2017 Schedule."
- 2019 Pro Bowl. January 27, 2019.
- Cleveland vs. Baltimore. December 30, 2018.
- Cincinnati vs. Pittsburgh. December 30, 2018.
- Pittsburgh vs. New Orleans. December 23, 2018.
- Pittsburgh vs. Oakland. December 9, 2018.
- Los Angeles Chargers vs. Pittsburgh. December 2, 2018.

- Pittsburgh vs. Denver. November 25, 2018.
- Pittsburgh vs. Jacksonville. November 18, 2018.
- Carolina vs. Pittsburgh. November 8, 2018.
- Pittsburgh vs. Baltimore. November 4, 2018.
- Cleveland vs. Pittsburgh. October 28, 2018.
- Pittsburgh vs. Cincinnati. October 14, 2018.
- Atlanta vs. Pittsburgh. October 7, 2018.
- Baltimore vs. Pittsburgh. September 30, 2018.
- Pittsburgh vs. Tampa Bay. September 24, 2018.
- Kansas City vs. Pittsburgh. September 16, 2018.
- Pittsburgh vs. Cleveland. September 9, 2018.
- New England vs. Pittsburgh. December 17, 2017.
- Pittsburgh vs. Baltimore. October 1, 2017.
- Minnesota vs. Pittsburgh. September 17, 2017.
- Pittsburgh vs. Cleveland. September 10, 2017.
- Pittsburgh vs. Carolina. August 31, 2017.
- Atlanta vs. Pittsburgh. August 20, 2017.
- Pittsburgh vs. New York Giants. August 11, 2017.

NFL Scouting Combine (nflcombine.net). Accessed on March 7, 2019.

NFL Throwback. "JuJu, James Conner, & 2017 Rookies Journey from Combine Prep to the Draft." YouTube (youtube.com). February 12, 2019.

NFL UP! Ambassador. "Combine Prep: A Typical Training Day for an NFL Prospect." NFL (nfl.com). February 20, 2015.

Nicolaou, Chris. "SCB Steelers' 2017 Training Camp Review: Running Backs." Steel City Blitz (steelcityblitz.com). July 30, 2017.

oaklandzoo12. "McDowell (PA) RB/DE James Conner Commits to Pitt." SB Nation: Cardiac Hill (cardiachill.com). August 13, 2012.

"Orange Bowl Courage Award." Football Writers Association of America (sportswriters.net). Accessed on March 26, 2019.

Patterson, Chip. "Watch: Pitt's James Conner Meets Eric Berry on the Ellen Show." CBS Sports (cbssports.com). April 21, 2016.

Pitt LiveWire. YouTube (youtube.com).
- "Football | James Conner Postgame | Duke." November 19, 2016.
- "Football | James Conner & Offense | Postgame vs. Penn State." September 10, 2016.
- "Extended Highlight | Pitt Beats No. 23 Notre Dame, 28-21." November 14, 2013.

"Presque Isle State Park." Pennsylvania Department of Conservation and Natural Resources (dcnr.pa.gov). Accessed on March 20, 2019.

Renner, Michael. "NFL Players of the Month - October." (Pro Football Focus (profootballfocus.com). November 1, 2018.

Quinn, Sam. 247 Sports (247sports.com).
- "James Conner Calls Ryan Shazier His Biggest Inspiration." March 22, 2018.
- "James Conner Is an Early Standout at Training Camp." July 30, 2017.

Schalter, Ty. "Rookie Minicamps, Where NFL Dreams Begin—and End." Bleacher Report (bleacherreport.com). May 7, 2015.

Shanker, Jared. "One Year after Lymphoma Diagnosis, Pitt RB James Conner Declares for NFL Draft." ESPN (espn.com). December 10, 2016.

Strackbein, Noah. "Pittsburgh Steelers Release First Depth Chart of 2017." Still Curtain (stillcurtain.com). August 8, 2017.

Staff Reports. "Conner to Wear No. 30 with Steelers." GoErie (goerie.com). May 10, 2017.

"The World's Toughest Job Interview?" *Gridiron Magazine* (gridiron-magazine.com). Accessed on May 22, 2019.

Thomas, Jeanna. "Ryan Shazier Injury: What Happened to the Steelers LB and How's His Recovery Going." SBNation (sbnation.com). May 4, 2019.

University of Pittsburgh Athletics (pittsburghpanthers.com).
- 2016 Football Schedule. Accessed on March 4, 2019.
- 2015 Football Schedule. Accessed on March 4, 2019.
- 2014 Football Schedule. Accessed on March 9, 2019.
- 2013 Football Schedule. Accessed on March 5, 2019.
- Pitt vs. Northwestern. December 28, 2016.
- Syracuse vs. Pitt. November 26, 2016.
- Duke vs. Pitt. November 19, 2016.
- Pitt vs. Clemson. November 12, 2016.
- Virginia Tech vs. Pitt. October 27, 2016.
- Pitt vs. Virginia. October 15, 2016.
- Marshall vs. Pitt. October 1, 2016.
- Pitt vs. North Carolina. September 24, 2016.
- Pitt vs. Oklahoma State. September 17, 2016.
- Penn State vs. Pitt. September 10, 2016.

- Villanova vs. Pitt. September 3, 2016.
- Youngstown State vs. Pitt. September 5, 2015.
- Houston vs. Pitt. January 2, 2015.
- Pitt vs. Miami. November 29, 2014.
- Syracuse vs. Pitt. November 22, 2014.
- Pitt vs. North Carolina. November 15, 2014.
- Duke vs. Pitt. November 1, 2014.
- Georgia Tech vs. Pitt. October 25, 2014.
- Pitt vs. Bowling Green. December 26, 2013.
- Pitt vs. Syracuse. November 23, 2013.
- Notre Dame vs. Pitt. November 9, 2013.
- Pitt vs. Navy. October 26, 2013.
- Old Dominion vs. Pitt. October 19, 2013.
- Pitt vs. Duke. September 21, 2013.
- New Mexico vs. Pitt. September 14, 2013.
- "Pitt Football Welcomes 30 NFL Teams for Annual Pro Day." March 22, 2017.
- "Conner Named Maxwell Football Club's Brookshier Spirit Award Recipient." February 8, 2017.
- "Pitt Falls to Northwestern in the Pinstripe Bowl, 31-24." December 28, 2016.
- "Pitt-Penn State Series Tagged as the Keystone Classic." August 26, 2016.
- "Pat Narduzzi Named New Head Football Coach at Pitt." December 26, 2014.
- "Conner Making a Case for Being College Football's Best Back." September 21, 2014.
- "James Conner." Accessed on April 6, 2019.

"Villanova Ranked in Preseason Top 25." Villanova University Athletics (villanova.com). August 9, 2016.

VisitErie (visiterie.com). Accessed on March 1, 2019.

WebMD. (webmd.com).
- "Benign Tumors." Accessed on February 28, 2019.
- "MCL Injury: What to Know." Accessed on March 2, 2019.
- "What Is a Biopsy?" Accessed on February 28, 2019.

Werner, Sam. "Pitt Players Say They Understand Paul Chryst's Reasoning." *Pittsburgh Post-Gazette* (post-gazette.com). December 20, 2014.

Werner, Sam. "Pitt Running Back James Conner Has Become a Favorite Son of Erie." *Pittsburgh Post-Gazette* (post-gazette.com). October 15, 2014.

"What Is Hodgkin Lymphoma?"American Cancer Society (cancer.org). Accessed on March 8, 2019.

"Young Boy Battling Cancer Meets Hero, Cancer Survivor James Conner." WPXI-TV (wpxi.com). November 23, 2016.

PHOTOGRAPHY CREDITS

ABOUT THE AUTHOR

Dr. Larry Schardt has been studying human behavior for more than 40 years. Being the oldest of eight, he's had lots of practice. He regularly shares his messages of inspiration, encouragement, and hope with audiences across the United States. He is known for his presentations on success, leadership, motivation, and happiness.

Larry was raised in Pittsburgh. He was brought up on the Steelers, Penn State, and Pitt. For 26 years, Larry has taught at Penn State. His classes include teaching, community, sustainability, and conservation.

Larry knows what it is to live without peace and joy. He overcame adversity, violence, and financial hardship. This enabled him to develop a "can do" positive attitude. He writes a daily inspirational Facebook blog in an attempt to celebrate and pay forward the positive in life. A few of Larry's inspiring life stories can be found in the *Chicken Soup for the Soul* series.

Larry can be reached via facebook.com/Larry.Schardt or twitter.com/LarrySchardt.